Writing the Pilot

By

William Rabkin

Table Of Contents

Dedication

This book is dedicated to the two greatest teachers a writer could ever hope for, Richard Walter and Michael Gleason.

Why Write A Pilot?

You've got a great idea for a TV series. It's going to combine the serialistic thrills of *Lost* with the sociological import of *Mad Men*, the blood lust of *The Walking Dead*, and the feel-good musical uplift of *Glee*. If you can get someone to read the script, you know without a doubt it will sell within an hour, probably with multiple bidders. If you can get it on the air, it will do what *Law and Order* couldn't and run longer than *Gunsmoke*.

But right now, your brilliant idea is still only that – an idea. What can you do with it? For most of the history of the TV business, the answer was simple: Nothing.

In fact, the real answer was worse than nothing. It went something like: *What are you, a moron? Networks don't buy shows from losers like you, so if you want to create your own series, go do what I did and get a TV writing gig, then work your way up.*

And if you think that's an exaggeration, then I'll quote no less an august voice than my own (although I choose to believe my co-writer, Lee Goldberg, actually wrote this passage in our book *Successful Television Writing*):

"If you have a great idea for a frozen dinner, you can't just send Swanson your recipe and expect them to let you cook it. We can scrawl a drawing of a car right now on a napkin, but it would be ludicrous to believe that General Motors is going to pay us to build it. So why would anyone believe that creating a TV series is any different?"

We went on like that for another page or so – I'll continue to use "we," although I must say that the tone of semi-outraged condescension does sound more like Lee than me – and ended up with the standard advice that the aspiring series creator write a spec script for an existing show, use that as a sample to land a job on a series, and then work himself up through the ranks until he is finally at a level where studio and network executives invite him in to pitch ideas. (A "spec" script is, of course, one written *on speculation* – that is, a script no one has requested, no one will pay for, and no one wants to read...) At that point he can open the massive desk drawer into which he's stuffed all the concepts he's dreamed up over the years and finally bring them out into the light.

With or without the outrage, that wasn't terrible advice when we wrote the book back in 2003. At that time, a spec pilot was still something of a feathered hippopotamus – a creature you could imagine, but whose use, desirability, or existence was highly dubious. Since there was no chance anyone would ever buy such a thing, the very act of spending the time and effort to create one tended to make the writer look like a clueless newbie, in the same way that sending out a spec episode of a show that had been cancelled two years ago would have. And it didn't fill the primary purpose of the spec episodic script, to demonstrate to a showrunner that the writer had mastered the most basic skill of the TV professional – to capture the voice of the show while still bringing something unique and essential of his own.

But there have been a lot of changes in the TV business since 2003, and several of them have made the idea of the spec pilot a lot more acceptable, both to those who hire writers and those who buy series.

And the biggest change of all is that spec pilots are now selling. At first it was just a couple of projects written by superstar showrunners like Aaron Sorkin – his first TV project since *The West Wing*, in fact – and J.J. Abrams, still surfing on the huge success of *Lost*. And for a couple of years after that, there was an occasional spec picked up by a network. But in the 2010-11 development season, the floodgates opened when the major networks purchased at least a dozen spec pilots.

Suddenly it's possible to create a script outside of the standard television development process and see it turned into a series.

Even if you don't sell your series, the spec pilot is an increasingly useful script to have in your portfolio. The reason for that is, quite simply, the stunning decline in quality of the dramas on network television. This certainly doesn't seem to be a problem for the networks themselves, as they keep putting on countless iterations of the same procedurals (*CSI* times three, *NCIS* times two, *Law and Order* times four, and that's not mentioning the endless unbranded copies). But for the showrunners and the creative executives at the networks and studios whose job it is to read scripts and evaluate writers, this has been a nightmare. And for writers who want to show what they can do, it's even worse. These shows are so rigidly formularized that even a produced example can demonstrate little more than basic professional competence.

And what's being developed seems to be less and less original every year. Even the pilots are getting formularized, with each new show borrowing its soul from an established hit, whether that means Dr. House transformed into a brain surgeon or a private detective, or *Gray's Anatomy*'s mix of sexual and professional hijinks transferred everywhere from a women's heath clinic to a spaceship.

Not that this is a completely new state of affairs. Television has always been an imitative medium – unless you think it's a coincidence that there were a dozen spy shows on the networks right after James Bond became an international sensation. But in the last few years as corporate control has tightened over the networks, it's gotten much worse.

Of course there is always the alternative of speccing an episode of a cable series. And it's certainly true that while the writing of network shows has been getting less and less inspired, that of the cable dramas has become more sophisticated with every season. Instead of focusing solely on valiant doctors, dogged detectives and brilliant forensic technicians, newer cable series tell stories about advertising executives confronting the damage their profession does to the culture, about a dying chemistry teacher turned meth dealer, about biker gangs and armies of the undead. Genres are still flourishing, but they're frequently turned upside down – crime solvers include a serial killer who preys on other murderers and a police detective almost as corrupt as the gang members he arrests. Even the less transgressive, more traditional, series like the "blue skies" shows on USA Network or *The Closer* on TNT have a depth of personality that hasn't been seen on the networks in years.

But writing a spec for a cable show presents problems of its own. For a spec to work, its readers need to have at least a passing familiarity with the series it's based on. If not, they have no way of knowing if the writer has gotten the voice right. Even worse, the reader will be thrust into a world of characters and situations he doesn't understand and will spend most of the read trying to figure out who is doing what to whom and why it should matter.

Granted, this is a potential issue with any episodic script. But it's a much greater problem with cable shows, simply because their audiences are so much smaller. *Mad Men*, which is frequently called the best drama on television and sometimes the best drama in the history of the medium, barely musters two million viewers per episode. Some only slightly less acclaimed series number their viewers in the hundreds of thousands.

Which means that a writer could spend months working on a brilliant spec for, say, *Sons of Anarchy* and find that the people he most wants to be read by don't know the show, and therefore are unwilling to read the spec or unable to evaluate it properly.

What this means is that there is almost no way for any but the most successful TV writers to express themselves creatively within the system. And while this may contradict everything you've ever heard about the business of television production, TV writers actually do yearn for creative satisfaction. Yes, we are paid obscene amounts of money to write exactly the same crap that fifty other people could do just as well, and when we're working, we love the job. But as the man said, there's no trick to making a lot of money if all you care about is making a lot of money, and as overcompensated as we might seem, we don't make a fraction of what a second-year investment banker can pull down. What we want from our writing is the same thing that the poets and essayists and fiction writers I work with in my MFA program want – to touch people. To make them laugh or cry or think.

In older times, the answer for these frustrated writers would have been to write a spec feature – that's where good, original writing belonged. But if network television has been dumbing down over these years, the movie business is actively plummeting into what can generously be described as a "post-literate" phase. Complex plots, rich characters, layered dialogue – no one wants them anymore. Films are being made for a global audience, and words just get in the way. What sells is pictures, and mostly pictures of genetically modified super-heroes and super-villains hitting each other over the head with slabs of concrete. There is simply no market for a drama aimed at adults – so why should anyone waste their time writing a spec feature that no one will want to buy?

(You can object here if you want: What about that brilliant drama that won a bunch of Oscars and made a fortune? It's certainly true that there are still a handful of smart, serious, important movies made every year. But for the professional writer – even the aspiring pro – choosing what to write next is a business decision as much as an artistic one. And the fact that someone out there is going to win the $375 million Powerball jackpot doesn't make it a sound financial decision to empty out your retirement accounts and pour the money into lottery tickets…)

Besides, even if there was still a market for serious scripts in the film industry, TV writers have gotten pretty sick of being told to look to a different medium if we want any kind of creative satisfaction. This, after all, is *our* business. It's what we do. Why should we have to leave television and spec features or write books – just because we want to do it well? The first waves of spec pilots were as much as anything a movement to reclaim an art form by and for the artists.

And while I don't have any way to prove this, I'd guess that first wave was written primarily to be read as writing samples. There simply was no expectation that a network would buy a script from outside its development process and put it on the air. Matthew Weiner, to cite what is still the most famous spec pilot ever written, has never claimed that he thought he'd sell *Mad Men* as a series when he wrote the script on spec; he was working on sitcoms that left him unfulfilled creatively and he wanted a sample that would show the producers of the kinds of series he wanted to write what he felt he was capable of. Indeed, he had his agent send the script to David Chase, who hired him on *The Sopranos*.

It was only after several years of work on what was then the most acclaimed series on television, finally rising to the level of executive producer, that Weiner took his spec pilot out with the serious ambition of having it produced. (In other words, he was following our advice in *Successful Television Writing*!)

The critical, artistic and commercial triumph of *Mad Men* – don't believe everyone involved isn't making money, no matter how small the audience – forever changed the way the spec pilot would be seen in the industry. It was obvious looking at the show that this was something that could never have emerged from any network's development process.

Which, it turns out, is what everyone wants right now.

You want proof of that? One statistic tells the story: All those spec pilots picked up by the networks were *purchased in January and February*. Which is to say, there was no great interest in specs at the beginning of the development season in the fall. The networks ordered their usual number of projects. They gave their notes at every stage of the process. And then, when the scripts came in that they had commissioned and it was time for the executives to decide which ones they wanted to shoot – they started buying specs instead. Because what they wanted was something that couldn't – and didn't – come out of their own process. No doubt these execs blamed the writers for the poor scripts, but to someone who doesn't wear the suit it's pretty clear that the studios and networks had noted and developed their own projects to death, and they needed to find new material that they hadn't yet destroyed.

All this goes to say why it's no longer a bad idea to write a spec pilot, no matter what those old hacks who wrote *Successful Television Writing* said on the subject. (To be fair to those hacks, there is a tremendous amount of information in their book that is still accurate and useful, and it should be read by anyone thinking about a career as a TV writer. Fortunately, it is still in print from John Wiley and Sons, and available for the Kindle. Download it now!) But before we move on to what goes into what a pilot is and what a great spec pilot needs, I want to talk a little about why a spec pilot is becoming more than just no longer a bad idea. Why it now is the most important thing you can write.

The Other Reason To Write A Spec Pilot

It's the terror.

No, not your terror as you stare at your blank screen and try to figure out how the hell to write the project you saw so clearly in your head. This, for once, is not the writer's fear at all.

It's the industry's.

You might not realize this if you're just looking at the bottom lines of the multinational corporations that run our entertainment business, but the entire industry is currently in a state of panic unseen in the last forty years.

Why this panic when there is so much money coming in? Becomes everybody knows that the entire industry is about to change – but no one knows exactly how or when. Television networks are losing viewers while an increasingly large share of the audience is watching on their DVRs or online or streaming to their TV. But Internet revenues are a fraction of what broadcast or cable ad sales bring in, and no one has a clue how to replicate that revenue stream. All they know is that these new viewers aren't as profitable as the older people in their Barcaloungers, content to watch the commercials as they wait for *NCIS* to return after this brief message from their sponsors.

TV networks understand these Barca-viewers. They've based their entire business model around them. And you might think that if these are the people who are happy with what the networks want to broadcast, the networks should be happy to appeal to them. But networks have spent the last thirty years convincing themselves and advertisers that the only people who count in this country are between the ages of 18 and 29. Apparently once you turn 30 – or worse, 50 – you will never buy another product or sample anything new again. So aside from CBS, which is quite happy to attract the largest possible audience, no matter who happens to be in it, the nets can only succeed if they attract a large proportion of the 18- to 29-year-old audience.

But the current generation of 18- to 29-year-olds doesn't watch TV the same way even those who have just aged out of relevance did. They watch what they want when they want, and most of the time they're doing six other things on their computers and eight other things on their phones at the same time. They've got access to just about every inch of film or tape ever broadcast in the history of television, whether legally on DVD or Hulu or YouTube, or less officially on pirate download sites. They've got no patience for crap they've seen before – unless crap they've seen before is exactly what they want.

The networks need to find a way to appeal to the new generation of viewers or risk losing the only demographic they care about. *But they have no idea what these people want.* And this is where the panic sets in.

Now you could argue that the reason they have no idea what "these people" want is that we're talking about a huge cross-section of the American public, and the notion that there's a single concept that will appeal to everyone who happens to text faster than five characters a minute is simply ludicrous. And God knows you wouldn't get any argument from me on that. But the fact that we both think this way pretty much explains why we're not network executives.

Hollywood has faced this kind of panic once before, when it found itself faced with a new audience who seemed to reject everything the studios had ever put out. It was just over forty years ago, when a movie called *Easy Rider* rattled Hollywood to the bones. A tiny-budget, European-influenced, plotless road movie about a couple of dirty hippies driving their motorcycles across America, it became an enormous hit. And the old men who ran the studios had no idea why. To them it was some piece of crap that violated every aesthetic value they'd held for decades. And yet, the new audience, which had adamantly stayed away from the multi-million dollar musicals and other road show behemoths that were currently bankrupting just about every studio in town, flocked to see it.

The executives were stumped, and they knew it. So they did what had never been done in Hollywood before – they threw open the doors. For one brief period, "any asshole with a beard" could get a meeting in a studio, and a lot of them ended up making movies. A handful of masterpieces came out of this period, and a few great careers were launched. But there was a lot of garbage, too, and a few artistes the world never heard of again.

This period didn't last long, of course. New executives were hired, ones who understood the modern trends in filmmaking and could separate the real talent from the frauds and wannabes. And of course a few years later, with the success of *Jaws* and *Star Wars*, studios regained control of the mass culture machine.

But still, that moment existed, and it gave filmmakers like Hal Ashby and Bob Rafelson and George Bloomfield a way in through doors that would normally have been closed. (Who's George Bloomfield? you ask. Exactly.)

That's where we are in TV now.

Okay, it's not quite as open as all that. You're not going to get thirteen episodes on the air just because you've got an iPhone.

But if you've got a fresh idea, the talent to pull it off, and the determination to fight until you can persuade people to read your script, you've got a good chance to be taken seriously. Because there's a desperate hunger for a new vision and unheard voice.

Now if you're not already counting your syndication millions, it may occur to you that this directly contradicts everything I said before – that the increasingly risk averse networks are sticking to a small and shrinking group of pre-tested talents to deliver reiterations of current hits. And, of course, it does.

But that doesn't mean both things aren't true.

Networks are always terrified of the new thing – but they're even more terrified that it will come along and they'll miss it. They need to be safe, but they want to be bold.

Which means they are tremendously attracted to a new writer with a voice that's truly unique, a concept they've never heard before.

Before you start sending out your scripts, you have to understand how few people are going to break through this way. The doors may be open a little, but they're still going to be barred to anyone who doesn't show extraordinary talent and who isn't willing to fight like hell to be heard.

But then, the film studios in the early '70s probably weren't nearly as open as it seems in retrospect. There were a lot more beards back then than there were development deals. Still, a lot of people got their shot who never would have if *Easy Rider* had bombed.

Some writers are going to break into television based on their spec pilots. There's no reason you shouldn't be one of them.

Or maybe it's closer to the truth to say there are a million reasons you shouldn't be one of them – but you are going to ignore them all, except for the ones you have direct control over.

And the most important of those is the quality of your script.

It's not going to be enough that it's good. It's not going to be enough that it's got a cool idea at its core. It's not even going to be enough that it's better than a lot of the other crap the executives read this week.

It's got to be great. It's got to have a bold, new concept that makes people see a genre in an entirely new way – and it's got to be executed flawlessly.

Sound easy? Sure. Because you're a great writer with brilliant ideas.

But what you don't understand is just how difficult a form the pilot script really is...

Your Great Idea For A Pilot

Both as a writer and a teacher of writers, I meet a lot of people who are certain they've got a great idea for a TV pilot. They want me to pitch it for them, or partner on the project, or take the whole thing over, sell and write it myself, and give them fifty percent of the proceeds.

You may be surprised to learn I don't generally accept these offers.

I'm thinking all the other TV pros these people have already approached declined as well. That's why some of them don't even bother with the business part of the project. They just launch right into the pitch, knowing that once I hear their brilliant pilot idea, I'll be so blown away I'll be desperate to join up. And before I can say a word, this is what comes spilling out:

There's this guy, he's maybe 25, about to get married to the most beautiful and wonderful woman in the world. But when they take a cruise together, she disappears off the cruise ship – and there's no record that she ever existed! As the guy searches desperately to find the love of his life, he must plunge into the depths of an international conspiracy.

This is where the writer stops, ostensibly to catch his breath, but really so I can ask that all-important question: Then what happens? Because he knows that if I do ask that, it means I'm hooked.

(And yes, I do know that the pitch above sounds suspiciously like a chunk of the pilot for *The Event*. It's astonishing how many amateur pitches sound exactly like *The Event*, and did for years before this show made it to air. Maybe that's why I barely made it through the second episode...)

There are days when I actually will ask what happens next, if only to see whether there's even a hint of an answer in sight, or if this is going to be one of those *Lost*-lite ideas in which every question leads to another question and nothing ever comes close to an answer. But either way, the pitch concludes and then comes the inevitable tag: *Isn't that a great idea for a pilot?*

And you know, a lot of times it really is a great idea for a pilot. There's only one problem:

There's no such thing as a great idea for a pilot.

You can have a great idea for a movie. Heck, the pilot idea this guy just pitched me sounds like one already, especially if he has any clue where to go after the first act. You can have a great idea for a novel or a painting or a twist on beef stroganoff. Because these things are all complete in themselves.

Saying you have a great idea for a pilot is like announcing you've come up with a brilliant notion for a chapter of a novel. It's not going to do you a bit of good unless you can figure out where you're planning on going with the rest of the book, and until you do you're going to sound pretty silly declaring yourself a genius.

Unlike a movie script, a pilot is not created to stand on its own. A movie's primary function is to entertain. The pilot shares that purpose, but adds another one that's just as important: It exists to act as the template for a series that can sustain for 22 or 50 or 100 episodes. 15 - templates conflicts that will sustain

If you're thinking in terms of "great idea for a pilot," you're basically focusing on aspects of the hour's story. *She disappears off the ship and no one admits she ever existed!* That's exciting, all right – but then what? Every week our hero is going to meet a new character who refuses to admit his girlfriend existed?

The real answer to the writer's question is: Yes, it is a great idea for a pilot. *Now what's the series?*

That's when you see the writer's smile disappear. The series, well, you see, the guy, he's searching for his fiancée and there's this global conspiracy and they may have kidnapped her and –

And again, we come back to the question: What's the series?

And if that's not hard enough, let's ask the one question that every executive asks after every pitch: What happens at the end of season two?

No one sells a pilot to sell a pilot. (Although the money is good...) More importantly, no one buys a pilot simply because they want that pilot. They want a series, and they're willing to invest upwards of a hundred thousand dollars in a script and possibly more than ten million dollars in production costs to see if that series is viable.

If all you've got is an idea for a pilot instead of an idea for a series, there's nowhere to go once that money is spent.

But what's the difference? How can you tell if your great idea works for a series or just for a pilot? In the next chapter we're going to explore exactly what a pilot is and what it needs to have a chance at success.

But for this discussion, let's look at one great pilot idea that turned out to be a terrible concept for a series.

Life on Mars may be one of the great pilot pitches of all time: Hard-charging police detective Sam Tyler is trying to rescue his partner (and fiancée!) from a serial killer when he's hit by a speeding police car. He's knocked out, and when he wakes up, he finds he's in 1973. And he's not just there, he seems to belong there. He's wearing period clothing, he's got a 1973 NYPD ID and badge and keys to a Chevelle. And when he gets to the station he learns they've been waiting for him as a transfer from another precinct. Now he has to find his way in a world with no computers, no cell phones, and no DNA – and in which the police are a lot closer to vigilantes than the professional force he's been a part of. While he tries to figure out if he is dreaming or if he's actually gone back in time, he finds himself investigating a series of crimes with eerie echoes of his present-day cases.

Cool, isn't it? Just from this paragraph you can see the pilot unspooling in front of your eyes. Scene after scene comes to mind, and every fish-out-of-water moment you think of summons up a dozen more. It's not hard to see why ABC bought this.

Except, of course, that there's no series here.

You may want to disagree. You may be able to spin out three or four stories right off the top of your head. Good stories, strong stories, stories that spring directly from the protagonist's central problem.

That's great – but the American financial model for series production doesn't allow for a show that lasts four episodes. If it's cancelled after one 22-episode season, it's a flop.

This is why development executives always ask that one question: What happens at the end of season two? Because they need to know your idea can sustain not three or four stories, but 44 or 66 or 100.

You might still think I'm not being fair to *Life on Mars*. Just because we can't come up with two seasons worth of stories right off the bat, that's no reason to assume we couldn't if we were given a reasonable amount of time.

But that's not what I'm basing my judgment on at all. I'm going by the pitch itself.

What works about this pitch, what makes it so exciting, is that it's a terrific *story*. You hear the hook and you immediately respond the way you would to the beginning of any good story: You want to know what happens next.

But a pilot isn't about the story. It's about the *conflicts*.

A TV series doesn't exist to tell one long story. It isn't a serialized novel. There has never been a long-running series that started with an outline for a beginning, middle and end to play out over a set of seasons.

The way a series works is not to follow one story, but instead to *explore a set of conflicts* that have been established in the pilot. These can be conflicts between the main characters, or between the protagonist and his world, or between clashing world views. Whatever they are – and we will be discussing the types of central conflicts in much greater detail very shortly – they will provide the basis for every story, no matter how long the series runs.

So let's step away from the very cool story of the *Life on Mars* pilot and look at the conflicts that would need to sustain the series through its five-season run. What are they?

Let's start with the obvious one: Sam is a man out of time. His 21st-century way of doing things clashes directly with the 1973 style of his colleagues. That's a strong, clear conflict. Or at least it is for maybe half a dozen episodes. But what happens after that? If Sam is smart – and Sam is going to be smart, because the leads of American cop shows are never allowed to be be stupid, at least when it comes to police work – he's going to figure out after a few weeks that he is in the 1970s, and that many of the tools he's grown used to working with are not going to be available to him. And if he doesn't, we're going to get pretty tired of him. The fifth time he calls for a CSI team to collect DNA only to be met with baffled looks, I know I'm ready to give up on the character – aren't you?

That still leaves the clash of police cultures. The 1970s cops are much more violent, much less professional – more like a posse than a modern force. Sam's methods will always be clashing with theirs.

Okay, so there's an actual conflict there. But it's not enough to stick any old conflict in the center of a series – it's got to have some kind of resonance with viewers. Is there any real debate going on in the country about whether we should return to 1970s-style policing?

Besides, locating the central conflict of the series in a clash of policing styles ignores the most striking aspect of the show's concept, the very idea that draws most of us to it in the first place: This isn't about two cops from radically different cultures who are forced to work together, *it's about a detective from the 21st century who's hurled back in time.* It doesn't matter how interesting you make the culture clashes, this is what people are tuning in expecting to find. The core conflict has to reflect that.

So what is at the core here? Well, one obvious aspect is to have Sam searching for a way to get back home. But how can he do that? He didn't run here through a time tunnel, so there's no secret tunnel entrance to search for. He didn't come in a time machine, only to lose the key. And he wasn't sent back by an evil wizard whose spell he needs to undo. He was hit on the head and woke up in the past; as far as he knows he's in a coma and dreaming the whole thing. So how do you craft stories based on his desire to get back to his home time when there's no mechanism for getting him there? *dead branches*

The other conflict they tried was to have Sam discover cases that resonated with events in his present day – he stopped a serial killer before he got rolling, he stopped the mentor of another incipient serial killer before he got that guy rolling. But how many times can you do this? After all, unless Sam was working on the Templars, Rosicrucians and Freemasons Global Conspiracy Task Force, how many of his 2008 cases could actually have anything to do with something that happened in 1973?

That leaves one last set of possible conflicts, and that is Sam's discovery of information about his own past that reshapes his understanding of his 21st-century existence. And that really does sound like it could provide some really interesting storylines.

Except that the accident that sent Sam back in time happened in 2008. (The series aired in the 2008-09 season.) Sam was sent back to 1973. That's 35 years. The actor who played Sam was 36 when this was filmed, so it's not too much of a stretch to suggest that the character was the same age, give or take a couple of years. Whatever Sam discovers about the life he lived back then happened before he was out of diapers. What's to discover?

The more you dig beneath the surface of *Life on Mars*, the more you realize that there's no series there, just a really cool idea for a pilot. ABC should have realized this when they heard the pitch, but they were apparently so swept away by the story they committed to a pilot, and based on that, to a series order. Not surprisingly, the first episode got a pretty good sampling from the audience – because it is indeed a cool idea. But that audience dwindled with every passing week as viewers realized what the network should have known the second they heard the idea: that there was no series here.

Two quick notes before we move on to pilots that really do

work:

If you doubt me when I say there was no central conflict to drive this series, you need look no further than the final episode, in which the executive producers were kind enough to wrap up the storyline for those few devoted fans who were still watching. A finale is, of course, where you resolve the story's conflicts. And what happened here? It was revealed that Sam's 1973 existence was all a dream – but so was his 2008 life! He was actually an astronaut in hibernation as he and several crew mates made the long journey to Mars. Which meant, ultimately, that there really was nothing to resolve here, and thus nothing to have explored.

And if you think I'm using the benefits of hindsight to claim superior insight to the entire executive corps at a major broadcast network, I can safely say that I knew there was no series here before ABC even heard the pitch. Because I'd seen the proof. *Life on Mars* was actually a remake of a British show, and it had all the basic problems of the American version.

You could contend that the British series was actually something of a hit, running for two seasons. But those British seasons each consisted of six episodes. Together they were barely more than half of one American season. And the original show, which did have a great pilot, ran out of creative steam about four episodes in...just like ours.

The Franchise

Before we move on, let me preemptively answer one question you may be asking: Does this mean we don't have to worry about a story for our pilots? Can we just start writing?

That answer, as I suspect you already know, is a resounding no. The pilot story will be crucial to your script's success, and we'll be discussing its crafting in a little while.

It's not that the story isn't important. It's just that it isn't the most important element as you're conceiving your pilot.

So what is?

This is where we get to the crucial difference between a pilot and any other kind of dramatic writing. Because the key element of your pilot is something you'll never have to consider if you're writing a feature or a novel or an epic poem.

It's called the *franchise*.

This is probably a word you've never used in conjunction with your writing before. If it's crossed your lips at all, it was probably in reference to a fast-food outlet. What could the local Burger King have to do with your script?

Everything.

I want you to think about that Burger King for a moment. Got it in your head? Good. Then quickly, what's the name of their signature burger? What's in their color palette? Do they dispense Coke or Pepsi products?

That was a trick question – but only because you really didn't have to think for a moment. Or at all. You knew the answer to every one of these questions instinctively.

(If you didn't – congratulations. You will probably live longer than everyone else reading this book right now…)

You knew the answers because Burger King has spent millions of dollars establishing its brand. The instant you hear the name, you know exactly what you're going to see and smell and taste when you go to one of their outlets. And just as importantly, you know what you won't get – a Big Mac or a Double Double or whatever those square things Wendy's sells are called.

Now I'd like you to think of a TV drama for a moment. Let's go with *Law and Order* – true, it's not in production anymore, but it had twenty years to establish its own brand, and it's one series that everyone has seen at least a couple of times.

Got the show in your head? Good. Quick: Who are the protagonists? What kinds of cases do they take on? What happens in the second half of every episode? What sound do you hear at the beginning of every scene?

You know all this, just like you know that Burger King sells the Whopper. And you know a lot more than this, as well. You know what socioeconomic bracket the stories are going to take place in, that of the rich and the powerful. You know how the first act is going to play out, with a series of quick scenes of the cops following leads until a suspect is arrested before the commercial. You know that one of the assistant DAs will clash over principles and procedures with the boss. You know the teaser will end with a witty quip by one of the detectives. You know that act three will almost certainly end with the key piece of evidence for the prosecution being thrown out. You know that the police detectives respect the prosecutors but are frustrated by legal maneuvers that keep them from doing their jobs. You know that the prosecutors admire the cops, but wish they better understood legal procedures so that fewer pieces of evidence could be thrown out by judges. You know that the judges are fair and impartial and give equal weight to prosecution and defense, ruling strictly on the law and the legal arguments in front of them, even when that means a truly despicable person might go free.

And you know so much more than this. You instinctively understand the show's rhythm and style and tone.

And mostly what you know is that you're going to find all this in an episode of *Law and Order* – and you're going to find something completely different in any other series about cops solving murders in New York City, whether that's *CSI: New York* or *NYPD Blue* or even the other two *Law and Order* shows set in Manhattan, *Special Victims Unit* and *Criminal Intent*.

This collection of everything that defines an episode of *Law and Order* is the franchise. And here are a few elements it contains:

The characters.

The setting.

The types of stories told.

The style of dialogue.

The way people interact.

The storytelling style.

All of these are hugely important in defining your pilot, and we're going to be looking at all of them shortly. But before we do, there is one thing missing from this list which is actually the most essential element of them all. The piece that will make or break your idea for a series.

If you're having trouble thinking what that might be, recall the key problem crippling *Life on Mars*. It was the lack of a central conflict to drive the episodes.

That conflict is the crucial element of the franchise. If it's not there, it doesn't matter how clever your idea might sound or how brilliant your writing. There is no series and thus no pilot.

But what defines this central conflict? And how do you know if it's strong enough to sustain a series?

To answer that question, let's look at a few that worked...

The Conflict

All TV series are powered by a set of central conflicts that drive every story and define the lives of its characters. You know this, if not intellectually then at least instinctively, because you're tuning in every week to see those conflicts engaged and resolved. What may not be so apparent is that there are two types of conflict in a show's franchise, and any series needs both of them to thrive.

The first type of conflict is the obvious one that provides the show's basic premise: The cops need to stop the crooks, the crash survivors need to get off the island, the advertising executives need to land accounts, the lawyer needs to win cases. These are the ones that are built into the series' conception, and it's a given that every story for a series is going to involve some variation on this basic conflict.

But just as importantly, every successful series has a second, deeper layer of conflict underneath that surface level. And this is what gives a series depth and meaning, what keeps it going when a dozen other shows with similar surface conflicts have disappeared to Hulu Heaven.

Take *The Closer*, TNT's long-running police procedural, for an example. What is its surface conflict? Well, it's a cop show, so it's essentially about police detectives trying to solve murders and capture the killers. Since it is a specific cop show instead of a generic one, there is a twist on that plain vanilla conflict – LAPD Deputy Chief Brenda Leigh Johnson is an expert interrogator, so that the detectives are always searching for the right suspect whom Brenda can get to confess under her brilliant questioning.

That's a pretty straightforward conflict, and one that's hard to distinguish from a dozen other shows, past and present. You could give the same basic description and end up with series as distinctly different as *Lie To Me* or *Homicide: Life on the Streets*. If you've seen *The Closer*, though, you know immediately that it is nothing like either of those shows, or all the others the description might fit.

What separates *The Closer* from those other shows is the deeper conflict that lies beneath the surface, which in this case has to do with Brenda's personal issues. As a police officer, Brenda is practically a machine – efficient, unstoppable, ferocious; she's the Terminator of the interrogation room. But in every other area of her life, she's a mess. She doesn't understand people, can't relate on the most basic human levels, and is constantly baffled by the way the rest of the world lives.

Every episode of *The Closer* has two stories, the crime of the week and a personal storyline for Brenda. And it's the struggle between these two sides of her personality that drives the show.

This wasn't accidental – it was built into the DNA of the show. Writer James Duff created Brenda as an outsider, a Southern woman newly transplanted to Los Angeles, to emphasize her separation from everyone around her. This conflict was always intended to be one of the central issues of the series. It's what the show is about.

I want to repeat that phrase, because it is the most crucial thing for you to keep in mind as you're beginning to hone your own series idea: *It's what the show is about.* I hate to hit you with a word that you've probably been trained to think of as dirtier than anything they used to say on *Deadwood*, but the great purpose of the secondary level of conflict in your series is to convey the *theme*.

There, I said it. You may want to stop reading right here. You may think that theme is for school essays and charity benefits and that your writing is so good you don't have to think of something as musty and old-fashioned as that.

In fact, theme is what drives TV shows, what sets them apart from each other. You can't start writing your pilot until you can answer that simplest of questions: *What is my show about?*

I can already hear the objections: TV is about entertainment, not theme and symbolism and all that film school crap.

To which I respond: TV is not possible without theme. Because it is theme that gives coherence to a set of thirty or fifty or one hundred episodes — it is by definition a *unifying* idea, and here it's what makes all those separate stories part of one larger whole. It's what keeps the audience watching. And that theme is always expressed through the series' central conflict.

But I'm not going to convince you simply by stating this, so let's take an example. Let's look at the most theme-driven show of the last couple of decades — and one of the most beloved, too. Joss Whedon's *Buffy the Vampire Slayer* ran for seven years, just over 150 episodes. And every one of those episodes was constructed around the same simple theme.

If you haven't seen *Buffy*, or don't remember it well enough, let's start by looking at the surface conflicts that define the show. Actually, the big one is right there in the title: The heroine is named Buffy and she's going to spend the series killing vampires. So, human versus vampire, a new battle every week. Just by reading the title a little more closely we can figure out that the heroine has a name generally associated in pop culture with frivolous teenage girls, so that's going to add a layer of ironic context to the conflict — the heroine is a teenage girl who kills vampires. And if you look at the opening of the pilot, that's exactly what you get. First there is a voiceover laid on top of a montage of vampire-related objects: "In every generation there is a chosen one. She alone will stand against the vampires, the demons and the forces of darkness. She is the Slayer." And then we cut to the exterior of a high school. So we've pretty well nailed what the primary conflict of this show is going to be just from the title.

Once we actually move into the pilot's teaser, we get an immediate sense of what one of the animating conflicts is going to be: A teenage boy and girl break into the high school's science lab at night. He's hot to take her up to the roof where, presumably, he'll make his move on her. She's nervous that they'll get in trouble and doesn't want to go. They hear a strange noise, she's spooked, he makes fun of her for being scared. He assures her that there's no one there.

So far, we're in strictly routine horror movie territory, exploring the basic beats of a million scenes that climax in the bloody death of horny teenagers.

Then there's a twist – after she's sure there's no one else in the building, the girl transforms into a hideous vampire and sinks her fangs into his neck. End of teaser.

Did I say this brief teaser gives us an immediate sense of one of the show's animating conflicts? I should have said two. The primary is the clash between a normal, contemporary high school life and the fantastic world of demons and monsters. The other is essentially stylistic, and it resides more in the viewer than in the text – it's the struggle between the genre clichés that have been implanted in our heads through constant repetition and the ways the show will attempt to fool us by playing into and then against them.

Those are both important aspects of the franchise, but neither is enough to drive a series. Because, really, after a few episodes we're going to start taking it for granted that the normal, contemporary high school life and the fantastic world of demons and monsters co-exist, at least for the purposes of the show, and it's going to stop being much of a draw. And while seeing clichés exploded is entertaining, it's a style that quickly gets to be as predictable as the clichés themselves.

But of course we haven't seen the central conflict of the series yet – because we haven't met our protagonist. And even when we do, it's hard to tell how her own personal struggle is going to work here. Buffy Summers is a new student at Sunnydale High, transferred from an LA school where she was expelled after burning down the gym. She's here to start fresh, and the opening six or seven minutes of the first act are all about her learning how to fit into this new place. She's quickly adopted by Cordelia, the leader of the popular girls, although we can see she's immediately drawn to the outcasts like uncool kids Willow and Xander.

So far – if we ignore the teaser – this could be the opening of a John Hughes movie. But just before the end of act one, Buffy stops in at the school library to borrow a textbook, and the mysterious librarian Mr. Giles offers her what he thinks she wants – a dusty tome on vampires. He knows she's the Slayer, because he has been sent to act as her "watcher." "It's not what I'm looking for," she tells him and runs out of the library.

What's really important is what happens next: Nothing. (Well, technically some catty girls are gossiping about Buffy in the locker room, and the dead body of the boy from the teaser falls out of a locker, but since our protagonist and her sidekicks-to-be don't know about the act-ending action yet, for them nothing has happened.) Buffy goes outside, sits with Willow, and says she'd like them to hang out together, maybe even do a little studying.

You might not realize it on watching the hour for the first time, but what Whedon is doing here is setting up the key conflict that will power every episode for the next seven years. Can you tell what that is yet? Or should we move a little further into the pilot?

As Buffy is chatting with Willow and friends, Cordelia comes up and informs them that gym has been cancelled because of the discovery of a dead body in a locker. Slipping away from the group, Buffy breaks into the gym, studies the corpse and discovers the distinctive fang marks on its neck.

What comes next is the key scene: Buffy goes back to the library to tell Giles, who says, "I was afraid of this." It's Buffy's response that sets up the entire series: "Well, I wasn't. It's my first day. I was afraid that I was going to be behind in all my classes, that I wouldn't make any friends, that I would have last month's hair. I didn't think there would be vampires on campus, and I don't care." To which Giles responds, "Then why are you here?" She's honestly stumped, and stammers out, "To tell you that I don't care. Which I don't, and have now told you. So, bye."

Of course the reason that Buffy's there is that she *does* care. It's her duty to care, because she is the Slayer, the chosen one. She knows that she is the only person who can stop the onslaught of the vampires and save humanity.

But she hates it. She doesn't want to be a superhero. All she wants is to live a normal life, worrying about classes and friends and hair styles.

This is the conflict that will drive the next one hundred and fifty-some episodes of the series – how do you choose between your deepest personal desire and your obligation to the world?

Does this sound too simple to drive more than a hundred separate stories? It is simple – but all good conflicts are. A strong conflict needs nothing more than the necessity of a choice between two equal but irreconcilable ideas.

What's important in a central conflict is not that it be complicated, but that it is impossible to resolve, and that it can manifest itself in myriad ways. Ideally it will also become richer and more complex as time goes on.

Which is how this conflict works out in Buffy. If you see the earliest episodes, Buffy's struggles to balance her life are played out in a fairly obvious manner: She wants to date the cute guy, but her slayer side is going to get him killed; she wants to be a cheerleader, but she's got to fight a witch who's cursing the squad. But as the series goes on, Buffy's personal needs become stronger as she gets older, and the pull between her desire to live for herself and her obligation to live for the world becomes more emotionally difficult.

This is a conflict that can sustain a series because it's one that can never be satisfied. Had the series run until Buffy hit middle age, she would still be dealing with the same issues, only presented in new ways appropriate to her advancing years.

(Indeed, this was exactly the case for Jean Valjean in Victor Hugo's *Les Miserables*, who sought a comfortable life for himself decade after decade, only to give it up each time it was in reach because only by doing so could he right a wrong for someone else. Only in death was he allowed release...)

It's important when you're looking for your pilot's theme that you choose something that can be explored from a lot of different angles – remember, your goal here is one hundred or more stories.

If your conflict is limited – if your theme is too small – your series will run out of steam

Let's look at two of the first dramas on the FX network for an example: the gritty cop show *The Shield*, created by Shawn Ryan, and the plastic surgery melodrama *Nip/Tuck* from Ryan Murphy, both of which had long, successful runs.

The Shield followed the adventures of Vic Mackey, leader of a small, anti-gang strike force working out of a run-down precinct in the worst part of Los Angeles. The second most important thing about Vic was that he was corrupt – he made deals with gangbangers, he stole money and other valuables, he was brutally violent when it served his purposes. In the show's pilot, he murdered a fellow officer who was spying on him for the FBI.

But the most important thing about Vic was that he believed he was a good guy. Sure, he made deals with criminals, but that was to keep worse criminals off the street. He only stole from crooks, and he did it to help his family. And if he was violent, it was because he lived and worked in a violent world, and that was the only way to get the respect of the bad guys he went up against. As for killing the other cop, that was required for his own self-defense – but even then he knew it was wrong, and it tortured him for the entire run of the series.

This was the central conflict that powered every episode of *The Shield* – Vic Mackey acted like a bad guy in order to be a good guy. And that was the theme as well: How much evil can you do in pursuit of noble goals before you stop being one of the good guys?

Like *Buffy*'s, that theme could have kept the show running forever. Because there would always be new challenges that would force Vic to become dirtier and dirtier.

Then there's *Nip/Tuck*. A melodrama about a team of plastic surgeons, one in a difficult marriage and the other a single sex addict, the central conflict had to do with people who were physically beautiful but whose souls were hideous. The stories were all focused around the theme: What price is worth paying for physical beauty?

Maybe you can spot a major difference between this thematic

conflict and those of *Buffy* and *The Shield*. The conflicts in the other shows were centered directly on the protagonists – it was Buffy who struggled between desire and duty; it was Mackey who descended into evil to achieve good. But Sean and Christian, the plastic surgeons, took on cases every week in which the cost of achieving physical beauty would be borne by their patient.

There was more to each episode than the case of the week, of course, The show also followed the soap operatic lives of the two surgeons. But as the series progressed through its six seasons, it became increasingly difficult to locate the conflict within the lives of the two doctors, and the plot lines grew ever more outrageous – which wasn't easy, since outrage was one of the show's chief attractions from the pilot on. When the series relocated from Miami to Los Angeles in the fourth season, the move came with an air of desperation, as if the writers were searching for ways to keep it fresh.

In fairness, I have to say that *Nip/Tuck* was a huge hit for its network from the beginning until the end, and no matter how silly the show got, the audience stuck with it. I certainly don't mean to argue with success here. But if you watch a first season episode and then one from the fifth season, you can see how much harder it is for the writers to tell compelling stories that rise naturally out of the characters and the central conflict. If you perform the same experiment with either *Buffy* or *The Shield*, you'll find that the later episodes are richer and deeper than the earlier ones, and that the characters have become more complex and interesting as their worlds have become more developed.

Nip/Tuck is that rare example of a series with a flawed central conflict that actually managed to work. If we were talking about architecture, we could probably find the occasional successful building that has a deeply flawed foundation. But don't let the fact that a handful of extremely talented artists have managed to pull this off fool you into thinking you don't need a strong central conflict located in your protagonist that can power one hundred stories. You do – and anyone who reads your script will be looking for it.

The shows I've been talking about are all ones driven by strong characters. What about series that are plot driven – and that have a cast of fairly interchangeable characters? Are they also theme driven?

You bet they are. To see this for yourself, you need look no further than the most successful of these shows, *CSI: Crime Scene Investigation*. In every episode of that series, the characters are an afterthought, there only because, well, *someone* has to collect all that evidence.

The theme of *CSI* is right there in the main title and, at least in the early episodes, lead investigator Grissom would state it outright: It's all about the evidence. The evidence never lies. And nobody can do anything without leaving evidence. Even the erasing of evidence is evidence. We are always leaving tracks of our existence, and it's the CSI team's job to find them.

The Characters

The concept is crucial. The theme is vital. But there's nothing as important in your franchise as your characters.

The reason for that goes to the most basic rule of series television: Audiences might tune in once for the premise, but they will only come back for the characters. That's why the original *Star Trek* still works today despite its clunky effects and dated moralizing while much slicker science fiction shows are all but forgotten – because we love the interplay between Kirk, Spock and McCoy. And it's why even a show that seems to be as free from characterization as *CSI* sees its ratings plunge when the actor playing the lead leaves – people really wanted to watch Gil Grissom.

If you have any doubt about this, you need look no further than a recent ABC show called *Flash Forward*. (Yes, another failed science fiction show on ABC...) It had one of the most arresting premises of any series since *Lost,* the one whose success it was designed to emulate: On October 6, 2009, just about every human being on Earth lapses into unconsciousness for exactly two minutes and seventeen seconds. During that period, the vast majority of them have a brief "flash forward," a vision of something that is going to happen in their lives on April 29, 2010.

Wow. That's got just about everything you could want in a premise. The one response we storytellers want more from an audience than any other is that most primal of all questions: *Then what happens?* And this is full of *then what happens?*

Just reading the synopsis starts raising the questions that are going to keep the audience hooked long after the pilot. Why did everyone black out? Why did they all have a vision of the same moment in the future? Will those premonitions all come true, or is it possible to change the future – if this actually was the future they were seeing? Is there some mysterious force behind the blackouts, or was it created by people – and in either case, to what end?

As I type these questions, I find myself getting as excited about the show as I was when I first heard about it. Then I remember...

What I remember is how thrilling that pilot was. Imagine what would happen if everyone blacked out at once – drivers on the freeway, pilots landing passenger jets, surgeons in mid-operation, soldiers caught in a firefight. There would be chaos, mass destruction, death and injuries on an unimaginable scale.

The pilot delivered all of that. It gave the audience everything we wanted and left us desperate for answers to all the questions it had planted in our heads. I can't speak for anyone else, but I was ready to watch for six years.

And then the actual series got under way. And we met the characters who would populate the show. First was crack FBI agent Mark Benford, who would lead the investigation into the blackout, and his partner Special Agent Demetri Noh. Then there was Benford's wife Olivia, a surgeon, their young son Charlie and his hot 19-year-old babysitter Nicole.

As far as their occupations go, this group doesn't seem badly chosen. You've got a couple of characters who will be right in front of the storytelling, and then a few more who can show how the blackout affects the rest of the world.

But aside from that, this may be the dullest group of characters ever assembled for a TV show. They are glum, troubled, passive and weak.

But here's the kicker – it would be just about impossible to create a set of characters for this franchise who *weren't*.

To explain this, we have to take a moment out to examine exactly how characters are created and defined in a dramatic medium. There are a lot of people out there – many of them in executive suites – who will tell you that the key to creating a character is to make him "likable" or "relatable." Or to give him clever little quirks. A special talent. A wry sense of humor.

There's nothing wrong with any of that advice. Except that none of it gets to the heart of what defines a character: his goal and the choices that he makes in trying to obtain it. Everything else is just talk.

Does that sound too simple? Let's look at one familiar TV character and see how he is defined – Don Draper in the first season of *Mad Men*. If you listen to his words, he's a successful advertising executive and a loving family man, devoted to his wife and children. And, at least in that season, he really seems to believe this description of himself.

We as the audience know better. How? Because every time Don is given a choice between remaining faithful to his wife and banging some cocktail waitress, Betty is left watching dinner dry out in the oven while Don is shacked up with the waitress in the Waldorf. From that set of choices we learn that Don is essentially dishonest, that he privileges his own pleasure over the feelings of those he claims to love, and that he spends his life lying to himself about what he really wants. If, when presented with the same options, Don made a different choice, we'd see him as a fundamentally different person.

Most writers have a pretty good idea who their characters are when they start writing. They know what kinds of choices their creations would make when presented with various situations.

The mistake beginning writers make is that, knowing all that, they neglect to put the characters in a position where they *need* to make those choices that will define them for their audience.

It's a fine thing to have a ten-page biography of your character in your head, to know that he's driven to succeed because his overbearing mother pushed him too hard when he was a child, that he only made it through the police academy because he cheated instead of studying and the knowledge he never gained ended up costing his partner's life, that he hates bad guys because his infant son was kidnapped and murdered, that he yearns to love again but is afraid to commit because his wife committed suicide after the death of their son, that he loves dogs and hates cats, that he believes that everyone lies, that his faith in technology eclipses his belief in people, that he slept with his high school math teacher. It's rarely possible to know too much about your characters.

But it's all useless noise unless you put your character in a position where he has to make a choice between two options, and we can see how some element of this enormous biography determines which choice he makes. You've got to put him on a street corner where a thug has just snatched an infant from a stroller. He's got his gun drawn and aimed at the thug. If he fires, he will definitely bring down the kidnapper, but there's a great risk he'll kill the baby, too. If he doesn't fire, the thug will get away with the kid. What will he do?

The decision he makes here – and at every other junction point he faces along the way – is going to define your character to the audience. And despite all the work you've put into crafting that biography, it will mean little to the people reading your script, because it can never have the visceral impact of seeing him make that choice. If the bio has value at all – and I'm not saying it doesn't – it's only in that it allows you to understand which decisions he'll make and why.

Which brings us back to the characters of *Flash Forward*. They come across as weak, dull and passive because there simply are no decisions for them to make.

This group of characters has all blacked out and seen a vision of their near future. FBI agent Mark Benford, a recovering alcoholic, sees himself in FBI HQ working on the flash forward case and being stalked by intruders – but also sees himself drinking again. His wife Olivia sees herself making love to a man she hasn't met at the time of the blackout. Nicole sees herself being held under water. Benford's partner Noh doesn't see anything at all, which leads him to believe that he's going to be dead before that day in April.

There's a common thread to each one of these storylines – not one puts a character in a position where he has to make a defining choice. Benford sees that he will have started drinking again in six months – what decision does that force him into? To pick up the bottle or not? That's not a particularly interesting dilemma, especially in a drama with a premise as big as *Flash Forward*'s. And there's simply nothing pressing about the question – at some point in the near future, Benford will decide whether or not to have a drink, and if he decides no, then he'll probably face that same decision again. At least Olivia's situation has a few more wrinkles in it, since she has to meet this man she's seen herself with and then make a series of choices about whether or not to let their relationship advance at all. But there doesn't seem to be much at stake at any of these points along the way, since the only serious decision is whether or not to have sex with him, and as far as we know that won't come for another six months.

The one set of decisions that Benford and Olivia do have to confront is whether or not to tell their spouses about what they saw in the future. Both choose not to – over and over and over again – and since characters are defined by the choices they make, both come across as spineless cowards, too scared of their own actions to even have an honest conversation.

And what of Nicole, victim of a violent crime by a stranger, and Noh, apparently killed sometime in the next six months? Both are in the same position: Since they don't understand what they're seeing – or not seeing – they are in no position to do anything about it. So all they can do is worry and, in Noh's case, whine. They are the definition of the passive character.

Was there ever a way to get around this problem in the conception of *Flash Forward*? It's hard to see one, because the very idea of the series entails waiting for six months to see if what people saw really has to come true. They're not given a series of benchmarks along the way to compare themselves to, they're not given a set of options to choose between.

Of course it doesn't help that most of the visions the characters see involve them being the victims of someone else's actions – Benford's getting attacked by ninjas, Nicole's being strangled,

Olivia's somehow being pressed into cheating on her husband. They can't make positive choices to avoid or embrace these futures because they have no understanding of who or what it is that is acting on them.

There is one character who is positively affected by his vision, and that's a dying cancer patient who is about to commit suicide to avoid his painful death when the blackout hits. He sees himself alive and happy in the flash forward, and on waking decides to keep living. And indeed, he discovers within a few episodes that his cancer has gone into remission.

But even this happier future is one that requires no choice on the character's part. He's not doing anything to put the cancer in remission, and the only decision he has to make to assure his future is not to kill himself – a choice he's made halfway into the pilot.

All this helps to explain why *Flash Forward*, which looked like a major hit in its first episodes, saw its audience dwindle away every week until it was finally cancelled at the end of its first season. Weeks after it left the airwaves it had been almost completely forgotten.

But we should remember the show for a little while longer, because it teaches a crucial lesson about developing characters for a successful pilot: It doesn't matter how "likeable," "relatable" or "interesting" your characters may be, *they will only serve your needs if they directly embody the conflicts inherent in your franchise.*

The protagonists of *Flash Forward* simply could not achieve that goal because the conflicts themselves were so vague and abstract – were the visions of the future written on stone, or could they be changed? Since no one knew what steps would lead to this future, there was no way for characters on either side to take action to confirm or refute the prophecies.

The series that *Flash Forward* was meant to emulate handled its characters in a much more sophisticated manner, and that show's success was a result. *Lost* was built around a series of baffling mysteries and never-to-be-answered questions, just as *FF* was, but it was also about something other than the audience's hope for the answers the plot might provide. The central conflict in *Lost* was between knowledge and faith, scientific certainty versus mystical belief. And because there was a strong philosophical conflict there, the creators were able to build characters that embodied the two sides in medical doctor Jack Shepard and formerly paralyzed mystery man John Locke, and then put them in opposition every week.

(Author's confession: I can't guarantee that this was the conflict that powered the entire series, as I have an allergy to the type of storytelling that keeps throwing out questions instead of answering some that have already been posed, so I bailed on the show after the first season...)

Once again, we must return to the fact that a TV pilot and its resulting series need to be governed by a theme, a unifying or dominant idea. The theme determines the central conflict, and that central conflict must be embodied in the lead characters.

In order to create compelling and effective characters for your pilot, you need to know what your series is about. If you want to write a show that's going to argue that the legal system has been reduced to nothing more than a game for its participants, with the general public their pawns and their victims, then you already know a lot about the kinds of characters you'll need to populate your pilot. First of all, you're going to need people who work inside that legal system – creating a show with this theme and then enlisting a doctor as your protagonist isn't going to get you very far. More specifically, you're going to need lawyers who believe the system is nothing more than a game – which you're probably going to find in the private sector rather than, say, the public defender's office, where the stakes are inevitably more personal. And these lawyers should probably be extremely successful, raking in millions of dollars a year and representing clients who are wealthy and powerful, because if you're aiding a client whose entire life's work is on the line in the case, you're also inclined to take things pretty seriously.

So now we've got a show about high-powered attorneys at a major firm. How do we narrow it down further? We need a protagonist, and since our lead has to embody at least one side of the central conflict, he should be a lawyer who believes that the entire legal system is nothing more than a game set up for his own amusement. And then of course we'll need someone else in the firm who believes the exact opposite.

Now there's no need for us to actually create this show, since *Boston Legal* ran for five seasons on ABC. We can, however, go back and look at the early episodes, which established these conflicts so clearly. And we will see how these characters, some wild and wacky, some deadly serious, were created to embody aspects of this central conflict. (For an even clearer view of these conflicts, you should look at the last season of *BL* creator David E. Kelly's previous show *The Practice*, which introduced the later show's leads Alan Shore and Denny Crane in what was essentially a 22-episode pilot for the spin-off.)

Or we can look at a show like David Milch's *Deadwood*. A Western set in a gold rush town in what is now South Dakota around the time of the area's annexation into the Dakota Territory, its central conflict was a fight over the coming mode of governance: anarchy versus democracy. There were a lot of characters in *Deadwood*, but Milch centered the show on the two who would embody the sides of the debate, hardware store owner and sheriff Seth Bullock, who worked to maintain a state of order that would allow everyone to live and prosper, and saloon owner Al Swearengen, whose business thrived on chaos.

The rest of the characters added support to one side of the argument or the other, and there were some – the widow who had inherited a major gold claim and would have to fight to keep it from various kinds of thieves; the newspaper owner who hoped his gazette would be a civilizing force – whose relation to the central conflict could have justified making them the series lead. It's conceivable that the show might have worked that way. But Bullock and Swearengen each had a direct, personal investment in the series' core conflict, and their respective roles would put them in direct opposition week after week. Thus, they are the ones who should be in the lead.

The Supporting Characters

Of course, no series can survive simply on the appeal of its leads. In fact, while you construct your franchise around your protagonists, it's not uncommon for supporting characters to become the most popular part of the show. From Kookie in *77 Sunset Strip* to the Log Lady in *Twin Peaks* to Chloe O'Brien in *24*, audiences have fallen in love with a series' minor characters and forced their creators to elevate them into major players.

One reason supporting characters can take off like this is that they are seemingly free from having to carry the baggage of the storytelling. They exist to create problems, say funny things, act outrageously, and amuse the audience. Look at any regular part Oliver Platt has played in a series over the last decade and you get the idea – he's inevitably an adorable slob completely in thrall to his various appetites, whether they be for food, drugs, or sex, and he will do or say anything, so matter how "shocking" it may seem.

(If there are any film students reading this who are looking for a thesis subject, it might be worth tracking down the astonishing number of supporting characters on American television shows that are directly modeled on *Absolutely Fabulous*' Patsy Stone. You can start with any role played by Oliver Platt, move into those with Christine Baranski, and then broaden out from there.)

But that seeming freedom can be a trap for the writer. It is easy to fall in love with the supporting characters who can say or do practically anything while your protagonist is weighted down with the actual freight of the franchise. What you need to understand is that a character who is completely unbound by the needs of the series' central conflicts is not only a waste of space, but a detriment to your pilot. The reader might initially be amused by his antics, but it won't be long before we eagerly await that Monty Pythonesque five thousand-pound weight to fall from the sky onto his head.

That's because the job of the supporting character isn't simply to entertain – it is, as the phrase insists, to support. Traditionally one says it is to support the protagonist, but in actuality it is to support the franchise.

Like your leads, your supporting characters must all have a direct relation to the franchise's theme. This is most particularly true in the case of shows where the conflict resides with the main character, a *Buffy* or *The Shield*. Then your minor characters exist to pull your protagonist in either direction, thus externalizing what would otherwise be an internal conflict.

To illustrate right and wrong approaches to the creation of supporting characters, we might as well look at two very similar roles played by Oliver Platt in two series that aired on Showtime.

The first of these was in a series called *Huff* that starred Hank Azaria as a middle-aged psychiatrist going through a mid-life crisis. As created by writer/executive producer Bob Lowry, Craig Huffstodt is a lifelong healer who is thrown into a tailspin when a teenage patient commits suicide in his office in the pilot, and he spends the series trying to understand his place in his own life while compulsively working to heal his schizophrenic brother, dying mother-in-law, confused teenage son and struggling marriage. Platt played his best friend and lawyer Russell Tupper, who wallowed in drugs, hookers, booze and food, and whatever other pleasures might strike his fancy.

From this description, it might sound as if Tupper had a strong purpose in the show – he would be one more person for Huff to heal. But the shrink's other "patients" were all in serious need of help. Tupper might have been, but he enjoyed his life too much to want it. There was never a serious question of him reforming his lifestyle. So he became a kind of comic relief. Like the rest of the characters he demanded healing, but never for his serious issues.

He had no interest in giving up his vices, and Huff knew better than to try to talk him into it. Instead, Tupper repeatedly called on Huff to bail him out of sticky situations he'd gotten himself into through his booze- and drug-fueled antics.

Thus freed from carrying the weight of the show's real conflicts, Tupper took off as a character – and took the show with him. The writers seemed to fall in love with Tupper's antics, and the broad comedy of his storylines stopped meshing with the subtler style of the rest of the show.

This was not the case with another character who was drawn almost as broadly. Huff's mother Izzy lived in the apartment over their garage and was as irreverent and nosy and annoying as any wacky neighbor ever to help populate a sitcom. Like Tupper, she got into wild scrapes from which she needed Huff's rescue. But unlike the lawyer, she had a real role to play. So much of the show was about Huff needing to restore sanity to his own life in an insane world, and healing his mother was a major part of that, especially since she lived with them and was always able to toss grenades into the family's relationships. Tupper's behavior was so extreme and his interest in changing so insignificant that there was no way to seriously integrate him into the series' center.

Several years after *Huff*'s cancellation, Platt was cast in a similar role in Showtime's *The Big C*, created by Darlene Hunt, which stars Laura Linney as Cathy Jamison, a reserved, even repressed, housewife who is diagnosed with terminal cancer. Platt plays her husband Paul, who in the first few episodes comes across as a toned-down version of Tupper.

Like Platt's earlier character, Paul is a grown man who has never left adolescence. He's got the same huge appetites – although Paul's seem confined to food and alcohol and toys and sports and other legal pleasures – and the same basic attitude that life is meant for his own enjoyment.

But Paul has something Tupper never did: a crucial role in the show's franchise. When we meet Cathy, she is almost completely closed in emotionally. She lives by rules, desperately desires order, and wants nothing more than to have everything go precisely the way it is "supposed to."

At first blush, it's hard to see what Cathy and Paul have in common, and how they might ever have ended up together. But in the course of the pilot the relationship becomes clear: They were young when they got together, and over the years he has stayed a child while she has taken on a mothering role toward him. The two seem mismatched, but they actually complete each other – she provides the stability and responsibility that keeps him from, well, turning into Tupper, and he reminds her what it's like to be young and irresponsible…and why she's made the choices she has.

That's the equilibrium as the series starts. But as soon as Cathy learns that she's going to die within months, she changes. With her future stolen, she decides to start living only for whatever pleasures she can have immediately. She becomes impulsive, selfish, irresponsible – essentially she becomes a teenager. Which means she is turning into Paul.

This is where Paul becomes really crucial as a supporting character. One of the primary functions of a minor character is to provide a mirror for the protagonist, and Paul's reaction to Cathy's change is one of our key ways of understanding just what she is becoming. We measure the difference in her personality by the changes she brings out in him.

And as the series progresses and Cathy plunges further into her new lifestyle, he becomes a yardstick by which we can measure how far off her normal path she's gone. For instance, despite all of Paul's adolescent behavior, he is an adult in at least one respect: He is completely faithful to his wife. Even when Cathy throws him out of their house, he is devoted to her. And when he finally succumbs to another woman's seduction, it only goes so far as him drunkenly accepting a handjob in a parked car. Cathy, meanwhile, launches into a passionate affair with a painter who is working on a mural at the school where she teaches. And while Paul gets drunk like a sulky teenager, Cathy experiments with whatever drugs come her way.

In this way, the character of Paul has a real function in the way the series operates: He is the baseline from which we judge Cathy's actions. Without him there would be no objective way to see Cathy and understand the emotional ramifications of her actions.

(Certainly it's true that we don't give up our own moral yardsticks while watching a fictional character, and we are free to judge Cathy's behavior as we will. But when we see the world solely through our protagonist's point of view, we tend to accept his actions as normative until we are somehow granted another perspective. See, for example, *The Big C*'s sister series *Weeds*, another Showtime dramedy about a woman in extreme circumstances, this one created by Jenji Kohan. That show's protagonist Nancy Botwin, a widowed suburban mother of two young sons, starts selling marijuana to pay her bills, and the series follows her through a long series of increasingly disastrous decisions that lead her deeper and deeper into self-destructive, criminal, and sometimes seemingly psychotic situations. But because we see everything from her point of view or that of her family, there is no objective voice to mark the insanity of each move, and until she reaches one of her occasional moments of enlightenment — usually coming at the point where she realizes she has put herself and her family in immediate threat of bankruptcy, jail or death — we tend to follow her choices uncritically.)

Paul has another function as well. By living as a perpetual adolescent, he has forced — or allowed — Cathy to become the maternal figure in the household, taking on the role of the grown-up in every situation. (And despite her complaints, it is clearly a role that she relishes as much as Paul does his.) Once Cathy upends that equilibrium by acting even more childishly than him, he is forced to accept real responsibility for the first time. Then, when she finally tells him the truth about why she's been acting so strangely — one of the first season's conceits was that Cathy refused to tell anyone she was sick — he begins to move into the parental role It seems clear that as the show evolves, they will move toward a new equilibrium in which they are both adults and both equals in the marriage.

Thus Paul gives us everything we could want from a supporting character. He mirrors the protagonist, allowing us to see her in a way we couldn't except through his eyes. And he acts as a catalyst for her, forcing her to reveal herself by constantly putting her in a position where she needs to make substantial choices.

That last part, by the way, is probably the most crucial role a supporting character can play. Since we only understand our protagonist through the choices he makes, a supporting character who is able to force the protagonist to make choices is one who will greatly add not only to your hero, but to the storytelling of your pilot and your series.

But this is all retrospective analysis, understanding how supporting characters function by looking at the way they've evolved over the course of a series. In the next chapter, I want to look at how we go about creating characters to fit a franchise.

Creating the Character

It's easy to look at a successful show and see how the characters work to make that series succeed. And it's even easier to look at a failure and see the mistakes. It's much harder to sit down in front of a blank screen and figure out just who are these people who are going to populate your series. But that's exactly what you're going to have to do.

As you are first beginning to conceptualize, there are undoubtedly some things you already know – your protagonist is a doctor or a cop or a superhero or a drug dealer. You probably have some notions about the way he'll function – if he's a cop, is he borderline criminal like Vic Mackey or is he rigidly upstanding like Tom Selleck in *Blue Bloods*? You most likely have a lot of pieces of what he has to be simply because your concept demands it.

Even so, at this point your characters can still be anyone you could imagine. And while that may seem like a good thing, it's really a problem. You need to make basic decisions about who these people are, and if you choose wrong, your series won't work. Where do you start?

If you've been paying attention, you already know the answer: You have to start with the core of your franchise. What your series is about. Otherwise you're just sticking people into situations and hoping something pops.

Let me give you a real-life example of how this writer approached creating characters for a series concept and a pilot.

Several years back, my partner and I sold CBS a pilot based on a series of successful mystery novels by Aimee and David Thurlo about a Navajo woman FBI agent named Ella Clah who leaves the bureau to become a special investigator for the tribal police force.

How we came to discover these books is lost in the fog of time, but I do remember what attracted us to them: They provided a new way of doing a cop show in a location and a culture we'd never seen on TV. They also gave us a character we fell in love with. Ella was tough, smart, brilliant, and at home in two completely different worlds, the FBI culture and that of the reservation. We were lucky enough to pitch the project to an executive who had Native Americans in his family, and he immediately saw the potential of the project. The fact that it was based on a successful series of books gave us an added level of credibility, and the network commissioned a script.

Now you might think that because we were adapting someone else's characters, most of the work had been done for us. And of course, that's always the dream.

But the needs of a series of novels that appear maybe once a year are very different from those of a television show that has to generate twenty-two stories in a season. The Ella Clah books are procedurals about crimes that take place on the reservation, filled out with strong subplots about Ella's relationship with the other members of her family and her tribe. Each book has a set of intriguing storylines, but the series as a whole lacked an ongoing set of conflicts versatile enough to power our series. We needed to find something more.

The first thing we did was go back and try to understand what had drawn us to the books in the first place. I know I already listed the surface reasons above, but this inquiry had to be deeper – we had read lots of books that could provide a new approach to the cop show, and we didn't option any of the others. Something had reached up out of these books and made us *need* to adapt them.

This, by the way, is one of the most crucial stages in crafting your series – or any kind of script – and the one that is most often overlooked. Almost any creative work starts with an initial blast of an idea, whether it's a scene or a character or a conflict or an image or even a plot twist. (I once had an entire feature script pop into my head while watching a Michael Douglas thriller on Netflix simply because I was so annoyed at the sloppy plotting I was being asked to accept. About halfway in I found myself thinking, "Why is this so bad? Why can't it go more like <u>this</u>?" And an hour later I had a rough outline scrawled out on a legal pad. So thanks, Michael!)

For most of us, that initial idea is the most exciting part of the writing process – one moment there's nothing, and then, seemingly with no effort, there's a series in your head.

It's rare that one starts writing from the initial inspiration, no matter how thrilling it seems at the time. Even though it feels complete at the moment, usually the inspiration has only provided a small piece of the whole. Sometimes there's enough that you can sit at your computer and start working out the rest of it right away. More often it seems appropriate to jot it down in a note, and then just carry the idea around in your head for a little while – sometimes hours, sometimes months. Ideas like this are generated out of the subconscious, and a lot of times there's a lot more to it that's still germinating back there. You can't force this stuff to come out by logic or craft (although the process does get easier with experience). You've got to let it germinate.

Finally, though, you've got enough pieces that you feel ready to start pushing forward. In the case of *Ella Clah*, we had a basic concept, we had a lead character, we had a setting, and we had a general idea what an average episode would look like. That was enough to start seriously exploring the franchise. (And we also had a network that would be giving us money as soon as we turned something in – which always makes the creative process faster!) But we were still missing the crucial middle piece, the series' central conflict.

For some people, this is enough to start writing. Looking back I'd guess that it would have been enough for me in the earliest days of my writing career. But what I had learned over the years is that if you start writing based on those subconscious urges without taking the time to understand them consciously, you end up spending an awful lot of time writing a bunch of bad drafts as you try to figure out what it is you're trying to accomplish. It's much better to come to that understanding before you start writing – or even outlining.

So we went back through all the Ella Clah novels – I think there were probably six or seven of them then. (There are fifteen now, plus one featuring her mother.) We skipped over the mystery plots this time and focused on those aspects of the character that intrigued us.

As we looked over the passages we'd underlined, we began to understand what it was about this character that appealed to us so strongly. She was the Little Mermaid.

If you're under a certain age, you are probably seeing images of adorable Ariel cavorting with dancing crabs and singing fish and wondering what she could possibly have to do with a Navajo policewoman. But I'm not talking about the Disney version; Ella Clah was the Hans Christian Andersen Little Mermaid.

If you've never read that story, the basic outline does bear some resemblance to that of the animated feature, but it is much, much darker. As with Ariel, the fairy tale's mermaid rescues a prince from drowning and falls in love with him. Desperate to be with the prince, she goes to a Sea Witch, who gives her a potion that will turn her into a human. She'll lose her power of speech, but she will grow legs. So far, it's not too far from the Disney movie. But what the cartoon leaves out is that the process of growing legs will be excruciatingly painful, and that while she will be able to walk and dance, every step she takes will be like walking on sharp swords, and her feet will bleed constantly.

You might remember in the movie that despite her inability to speak, Ariel is finally able to convince the prince that she the woman he's been searching for. Not so much in the original. He believes he was rescued by a girl from the temple where the mermaid left him, who just happens to be the princess his father wants him to marry.

And so the Little Mermaid is cast out of the prince's house. She can't return to the sea, because she can no longer breathe underwater and she will drown. But she is an outcast in the human world as well – mute, friendless, and suffering unbearable agony with every step she takes.

The Little Mermaid is caught between two worlds, and she can never truly be a part of either one. She's left behind a world she knows and can't be admitted to the one she craves. Her life is a constant struggle between them, and she is an outsider wherever she goes.

And she is a perfect metaphor for the lives so many of us lead, torn between the culture we grew up in and the one to which we aspire.

That's what we had seen in Ella Clah when we first read those books. That's what had drawn us to her. We wanted to explore a character who was caught between cultures, a perpetual outsider.

Now that we understood this about Ella, we could go back and start figuring out how we needed to approach her character. Because this conflict provided the answers to most of our questions about the series.

What we realized was that the series' central conflict had to do with identity. The Thurlos' Ella had run away from the reservation as a young woman and eventually joined the FBI, but when she's sent back to Albuquerque to solve a murder involving a tribal elder, she reconnects with her traditionalist mother and realizes that she belongs back in her old home. At the end of the first book, she quits the FBI to take a job with the tribal police force, and that's her position for the rest of the series.

Again, that was a choice that was fine for the books. But it completely undercut what we hoped to accomplish with the series. We needed Ella to be torn, and the Thurlos' character had already decided where her cultural loyalties lay – she had thrown in with her heritage. That set the series in a point in her life after which she'd found the answers to the most difficult decisions in her life.

The first major change we made was to keep Ella in the FBI. More than that – we made the FBI the most important thing in her life. We wanted her not only to be a brilliant investigator, but a desperately ambitious one. She wants to make it to the top of the bureau, and when we meet her she's a rising star in Chicago. More importantly, she has given herself entirely to the bureau's culture. She walks, talks and thinks like she's never been anything other than Special Agent Clah. She has rejected the Navajo culture completely.

But there's a bizarre murder on the reservation outside of Albuquerque, and the call goes out for a special agent who can speak and understand Navajo. And in the FBI, she's it. Ella doesn't want to go, not only because she knows that when an FBI agent is sent from a big bureau to a small one it's nearly impossible to climb back up, but because she dreads reawakening all the feelings that drove her away from home in the first place. Indeed, as soon as she returns, she finds herself dealing with all sorts of issues she thought she'd finished with forever.

This was going to be our lead character – a woman who had through sheer force of will transformed herself from a Navajo girl into a special agent of the FBI. She has spent years excising every Native American aspect of her life. But now she's back in Albuquerque and on the reservation, and the only way she'll be able to succeed in her current life – to solve the murder and bring the case to a successful resolution – is to act, talk and think like a Navajo.

And of course at the end of the pilot, Ella will have been so successful that she is reassigned to New Mexico permanently, where she will have to deal with the same issues every week.

(You probably noticed this already, but we helped amp up our protagonist's conflicts by giving her a need to rise within the Bureau, something that's almost impossible to do from a small bureau like Albuquerque. That gave her a constant goal to fight toward – a promotion and transfer back to one of the major offices.)

Once we understood Ella this way, we felt we were half way done. We'd figured out how the series would work. We knew that in every episode Ella would be torn between her desire to have nothing to do with her heritage and her need to accept the Navajo culture in order to do her job. That told us what kind of cases she'd have to solve and what it would mean to her to take on each one. What it would cost her, and what kinds of choices she'd make.

But we weren't quite ready to start working out our pilot story yet. There was still a big piece missing.

Creating The Supporting Characters

Because we had figured out Ella Clah's central conflict, we were almost ready to start plotting out our pilot story. *Almost.*

The problem was that Ella's conflict was a completely internal one – she was torn between two cultures. And while an internal conflict is fine if you happen to be writing a novel or short story, it's death in a filmed medium. We can't capture our character's internal thoughts and feelings, we can't explore their mixed feelings. We can't dive into their innermost thinking, we can only show what they say and what they do.

(This is a mistake commonly made both by beginning screenwriters and independent filmmakers, who seem to believe that showing a character sitting on the edge of a bed and staring out the window will express anything other than the writer's complete lack of inspiration…)

This is not to say that film and television are shallow mediums, incapable of conveying a complex character, merely that if we choose to explore our protagonist's internal conflict, we must first find a way to make it *external*.

We knew how we would do that for Ella. Each of her cases would force her to choose between doing things the FBI way and using traditional Navajo methods, and that would be great for showing how she is managing to reconcile the two sides. But we also wanted to understand her thought processes as she reached each decision, and to feel the struggle that was going on inside her at all times. We needed to find a way to dramatize each side of each choice so that we understand what she's deciding between.

To do that, we knew we had to introduce a set of supporting characters, each one of whom would stand for one aspect of the struggle.

We started with the simplest part of the equation – Ella's ambition within the FBI. Inside of Ella, this is actually quite a complex set of desires, since it represents not only success in her chosen career, but the complete abnegation of her own culture. The Bureau has no room for personal expression.

But whoever represents her FBI ambition doesn't need to reflect that complexity, because we're going to have other characters to dramatize the issue. We need someone purely aspirational. If Ella had never left Chicago, we could have created another agent, possibly a white woman with the right background on the fast track to the top, and let Ella compete against her. But one of the reasons Ella hates being back in New Mexico is because a field office like this is such a dead end for an agent. The woman we're imagining here would never set foot in Albuquerque. So she's not going to work for us.

There are probably a couple of different ways we could go with this, but because of the simplicity of the character's role in Ella's conflicts, the simplest is probably the best. We'll give Ella a boss who is FBI all the way. We don't know yet whether he's going to be a friend to Ella or an obstacle, but his primary role is as the gatekeeper to the promised land. He's the one who can recommend her for a transfer back to Chicago, or New York or DC. He's the one who holds the key to everything she's ever wanted. We can figure out his personality later – his role is already set, so all that matters is that we find some way to draw him so he's a little bit different from all the other bosses on all the other cop shows. We'll figure that out once we start writing.

Then we need the side of the struggle that's pulling Ella back toward her Navajo roots. That one is easy, too, because Aimee and David Thurlo have been kind enough to create a wonderful character in Rose Destea, Ella's mother. She's loving and funny and infuriating in the way that only a mother can be. A huge personality, you want to spend time with her – but it's easy to see how such a huge personality could be smothering to a young girl like Ella. And in this case the smothering takes the form of trying to get Ella to accept her Native American roots.

Except this is not quite as easy as it first seems. Because Rose isn't there just to stand in for Ella's Navajo cultural history – she's got to be the subject of some extremely mixed feelings from her daughter. Remember, Ella has tried to wipe her past out of her life – and Rose is a big part of what she's tried to eliminate. They haven't spoken in more than a decade. What's driven Ella to such an extreme, and how can we convey this without turning Mom into a monster?

The books provide an answer. Ella's late father was a Navajo who had converted to Christianity and become an itinerant preacher, traveling over the entire reservation to spread the Gospel in a converted ice cream truck. As a child, Ella was caught between her two parents, each of whom demanded she accept their belief system in an increasingly violent series of altercations. Finally, Ella couldn't take anymore and ran away from both of them.

But Dad is dead when the books begin, and as we think about it these fights seem far removed from the story we want to tell. Which is going to leave Rose a very difficult character to write – she has to have been terrible enough to send Ella scurrying away from her entire heritage, but welcoming enough that there is actually some appeal to her repeated invitations for Ella to come back home. There are some gimmicky ways to do this – Mom was drunk all the time when Ella was a child but now she's sober, for a particularly dismal example – but we would prefer to avoid that kind of solution. We have a pretty good idea who Rose is, and we'll figure out in the plotting how she'll function.

(Which, by the way, is a terrible way to deal with a problem like this. Rose needs to be an integral part of the pilot and the series, and we were crossing our fingers and hoping we'd figure her out. Don't do this.)

One thing we did know was that if Ella's relationship with Rose was going to reflect the constant push and pull of her feelings, and would embody so much of the good there is for her to find in her native culture, we needed another Navajo character who could symbolize the *demand* that she embrace her heritage. We needed someone who could say the thing that we knew would always be in the back of Ella's mind – that she had betrayed her culture and abandoned her people by running away. That she owed it to her tribe to rejoin them and accept their ways instead of signing on with the government that, in a previous time, had tried to wipe them out. That she was not and never could be a real American, because she would always be a Navajo.

Again, we were fortunate that the Thurlos had given us this character, too. In the books Ella has a brother who is both a medicine man and a radical fighter for Native American rights. He believes that the whites have stolen America from their people, and he is not going to rest until he sees justice for the tribe.

I will confess, Ella's brother is not my favorite character in the books or in the script. It's hard to write a minor character as a political firebrand without reducing him to a series of angry speeches, because you've got to make clear that this is what he's all about and you don't have a lot of time to build in nuance.

But adding him to the mix turned out to be a great turning point for our conception of Ella's character and the series, because he fundamentally changed one side of Ella's conflict. As we started imagining her we saw the conflict between the desire for the FBI culture and the unacknowledged longing for her native heritage. What the brother added was something we'd completely forgotten about – the guilt that Ella feels about turning her back on her old life. And it gave us a person who could say what we now realized had to be in the back of Ella's mind at all times – that she had no business pretending that she could ever be part of the white world. It made her feelings about coming back so much more complex.

As we could feel the conflicts on Ella's Navajo side getting deeper and richer, it was becoming clear that her FBI side was far too simple. As we'd shown it so far, the FBI culture was the totality of Ella's goals and nothing more. We needed a way to explore the complexities of being a Native American woman in an institution that's hardly famous for cultural diversity – and we couldn't do it through Ella because she is not at this point in her life able to acknowledge to herself that there's anything less than ideal about her life in the Bureau.

Fortunately we hadn't yet given Ella a partner yet. Now we had a real role for him. We needed him to be a cultural exile like Ella – but to be self-aware in a way that she simply couldn't be. To be able not only to understand but talk about what it's like to be a minority in the FBI.

Obviously we didn't want another Native American FBI agent, since that would step on so many of Ella's conflicts. Instead we introduced Alfie Mardones.

Alfie is a third- or fourth-generation Mexican-American FBI agent who has spent his life battling the bureau's institutional bigotry and been exiled to Albuquerque as punishment. It's not that he's been fighting for special treatment as a minority – just the opposite. All Alfie ever wanted was to be the best FBI agent he could be. But the bureau leadership could only see him as "the Hispanic agent." They kept giving him assignments they knew he'd be especially well suited for, like monitoring the wiretaps of Central American drug smugglers.

This turned out to be a problem for Alfie. I mentioned he was third- or fourth-generation American, right? In fact, his family is so well assimilated that he grew up without speaking or even understanding a word of Spanish.

But again, to the bureau, he's the Hispanic guy. And no matter how many times he tries to explain the truth to his bosses, they are incapable of hearing it – and they accuse him of insubordination, finally exiling him to the Albuquerque field office.

(This may sound ludicrous, but in fact much of Alfie's character – including the bit about monitoring wiretaps in a language he didn't speak – was drawn in large part from a real, retired FBI agent we interviewed extensively before we started plotting. In the same way we were able to learn a lot about the Navajo tribal police force by interviewing a female officer who had worked there for years – and who might have been the Thurlos' original inspiration for Ella Clah, although neither she nor they ever said such a thing.)

Alfie became a great tool for understanding Ella. He mirrored her dilemma, but did so in completely different tone. She was agonized about her place in life; he was cynical, resigned, even amused. He could say the things she never could, the things that were too painful for her to acknowledge. He understood a lot of what she was going through, and was able to articulate the thoughts she couldn't acknowledge even to herself.

At this point we were really ready to start working out our pilot story. The mystery came together easily, and we found that the supporting characters did exactly what we needed them to – force Ella to reveal her character by constantly putting her into positions where she had to make choices.

We turned in our first draft of the outline and waited for notes. Our CBS executive loved it – mostly. There was one element that wasn't working at all: Ella's mother. She was funny and strong and overbearing, just as we (and the Thurlos before us) had intended – and he had no idea why Ella had such negative feelings toward her. Which created two problems. Not only did our first reader have no clue why Ella had run away from home and tried to wipe out every trace of her past – which was only the single most important part of her character – but he thought the way she treated her mother made her look like something of a bitch. Audiences would fall in love with Rose, and they'd hate Ella for not liking her, too.

Fortunately this executive had a fix to suggest. He had actually read the books we'd left behind when we pitched – something that still shocks me after all these years – and he'd fallen in love with the character of Ella's father. For him, the image of this old Navajo driving across the reservation in a beat-up ice cream truck preaching the Gospel was everything the show was supposed to be about. And as soon as he said that, we realized he was right. It was true that the character was dead by the start of the first novel, but there was no reason we couldn't change that for the series. We agreed to make the change.

We went back, tore the outline apart, and rebuilt it with Ella's father in a prominent role. And an amazing thing happened. Not only did Rose's character begin to make sense, Ella's came into much clearer focus.

We'd always known that the central event of Ella's life was her running away from the reservation. We knew that she had turned her back on her Navajo heritage. But we had always taken that as a given that needed no explanation – it just was.

But once we introduced her father – and, just as importantly, the relationship between father and mother – we not only understood what happened, we were able to see it. Ella's mother and father were both strong-willed people of tremendous faith. Unfortunately they believed in different faiths. They battled all the time, fighting for the supremacy of their beliefs. And of course their battlefield was… Ella. Throughout her childhood, Ella was the pawn in her parents' battle for cultural superiority, pulled in diametrically opposed directions. Until she couldn't stand it anymore, and she ran away.

Now Rose made sense. She could be loving and funny and only comically overbearing, because that other side of her would only come out in the context of her relationship with her husband.

More importantly, we had a much greater understanding of Ella. We no longer had to wonder why she was so violently opposed to the Navajo culture and drawn to that of the FBI. We could see that she had turned her back on <u>all</u> cultures and religions. She'd come to believe that they brought nothing but strife and hatred, and she wanted nothing to do with any of it. No wonder she embraced the FBI culture.

Once again, the introduction of a supporting character had helped to clarify and define our protagonist.

And what was even better, we had successfully populated our franchise with characters who would continue to push Ella to reveal and define herself. Our conflicts were equally weighted on all sides, and that would give us what we needed to generate *Ella Clah* stories for years.

The Rest of the Franchise

Once you have your concept, your characters and your central conflicts, you are almost ready to start figuring out your pilot story. But there are still a few elements of your franchise you might want to consider before charging forward.

First of these is the *world* your series will take place in. Or, rather, how you will portray that world.

Some of its aspects will have been determined by your premise – for example the kinds of locations in which your stories will take place. *The Shield* obviously required an urban setting – more specifically, an urban ghetto. *Law and Order: Criminal Intent* generally set its stories in the upscale Manhattan of multi-million dollar apartments, high-end restaurants, brokerages and galleries. *Ella Clah*, had it gone to series, would have been far more rural than either of these series, with stories split between the Navajo reservation – which is about as rural as any place in America, even where it is most developed – and the small city of Albuquerque.

(And if you're thinking that this is not a crucial decision, think again. One reason CBS ultimately passed on *Ella Clah* was the concern that it would feel too rural, which has been a dirty word on network television since Fred Silverman cancelled *Green Acres*, *Mayberry R.F.D.* and *Hee Haw* and replaced them with hipper urban shows like *All In The Family* and *The Mary Tyler Moore Show*. Another CBS pilot we wrote called *Hong Kong* failed because of concerns over shooting in China. Since both concepts were irretrievably tied to their settings, there was no way to change them to make them more acceptable, something that's a little easier if it's simply a matter of moving the locale from, say, San Francisco to Seattle…)

But there's more to your world than the geographical location. One of the most important factors is the way people relate to each other in your franchise.

This may sound like an odd concept. Different people relate to each other in different ways. And there's certainly truth to that. But your world is, like everything else in your pilot, going to be determined by your central conflicts, and your people are going to be controlled the same way.

The Shield, for example, takes place in a hostile, violent world. Not surprisingly, that world tends to be populated with hostile, violent characters. But it's got another effect as well: Since everyone here is subject to constant attack, they are all armored. Even in their personal relationships, they protect themselves from the dangers of the world outside. They don't share feelings, they don't talk about their hopes and fears, and they don't trust other people. Whereas in, say, *Glee*, people can't stop talking about their feelings and reaching out to each other.

Or look at *The Riches*, a sadly short-lived show created by Dmitry Lipkin that ran for two seasons on FX. A comedic drama about the real costs of the American dream, the show followed a family of "travelers" – Irish gypsies who live as itinerant con artists – who take over the lives and identities of a wealthy family they killed in a traffic accident and struggle to fit into mainstream society without being discovered as frauds.

Geographically the show is split. Most of the storylines take place in the upscale gated community where the "Riches" now live (and the husband works) – although we are frequently given views of the kinds of places they have fled, the camps of the Travellers and the lower-class neighborhoods where people with their actual social status have to live.

And the way people relate to each other is split, too. This is a tribal world, and everyone functions differently depending on whether they are inside the tribe or outside. To members of their own tribe – whether it's the wealthy inhabitants of the gated suburb or the Travellers' caravan city – they are friendly, or at least polite and considerate. But anyone outside the tribe is a mark – and that goes not only for the gypsy conmen, but the wealthy group who make their money in fraudulent real estate deals.

That is a constant throughout the series – it is, in fact, one of the things that defines the series. It may not be something you think out completely before you start writing, but it is definitely one aspect of the script you'll need to discover as you go along. Because everything you put forth in the pilot script is part of the template for the next hundred episodes.

Similarly, the pilot's style of dialogue is something you may actually find in the writing of the script. Just be sure you realize that every great series does have its own approach to dialogue, whether it's the intensely articulate (and intensely long) speeches of Aaron Sorkin's *The West Wing* – and please don't try this unless you are every bit as good as Sorkin – or the juxtaposition of clipped, direct military-speak and high-minded philosophizing of *Battlestar Galactica* or the ultra-hip teen slanguage that characterized *Buffy*. Give your show a voice.

There is one other element you need to consider seriously before you start plotting, because it will have a major impact on how your pilot will read. That's the style of storytelling.

Until a handful of years ago, this is something you wouldn't have wasted a moment contemplating. There was one storytelling style on television: You start at the beginning and you end at the end. Period.

That's still the dominant structural mode of many series, but it's no longer the ironclad rule it used to be. If you pick up a screenwriting manual from as late as the mid-'90s, you'll still see warnings that a flashback is the hallmark of the amateur writer, and guaranteed to make your reader hurl your script across the room. But over the last few decades, to paraphrase the late Kurt Vonnegut, TV has come unstuck in time. Every episode of *Lost*, for example, spent a quarter to a third of every hour in flashbacks to times before the plane crash – until the last few seasons, when they started devoting the same amount of time to flash-forwards to times after the crash victims had been rescued. Even as straightforward a series as *CSI*, which set the paradigm for just about every crime series on the major networks over a ten-year period, used flashbacks in every episode to reveal the truth about the crime.

Right now there seem to be no rules about the style of storytelling on TV. *The Event* runs in several different timeframes every episode; *Glee* pops in and out of various points of view, even stopping the action to get directly inside a character's head.

This is incredibly liberating for us as storytellers. But that kind of freedom comes with a price. What you need to understand before you launch into a script told from four different points of view scattered over a dozen centuries is that whatever choice you make, you're going to be stuck with it. And even if you are thinking to yourself that this is just a writing sample and that the odds of it getting made and you being forced to keep duplicating this structure one hundred times over are about a zillion to one, you need to keep in mind that the people who are reading this – even as a sample – will be judging your writing based on how well you've conceived your pilot. Maybe that doesn't seem fair, but it was your choice to write a pilot, right?

What you need to think through is just how your style of storytelling is going to affect the content of your stories. For a cautionary tale, I turn to the example of the late and much lamented *Veronica Mars*.

Veronica Mars was broadly considered to be the UPN network's attempt to follow the then-recently canceled *Buffy*. Like its predecessor, *VM* placed a cute, blonde high school student in the center of a genre that was traditionally dominated by adult males. In this case, it was the *film noir* detective story.

And what a story it was! Veronica Mars is a working class kid in an ultra-wealthy Southern California beach community. Even though she's not from their socio-economic bracket, Veronica is accepted by the elite of the rich kids because her father Keith is the sheriff. Her best friend is Lily Kane, daughter of software magnate Jake Kane, and she's even dating Lily's brother. Life is good.

But then everything goes to hell. Lily is found murdered by the family pool. And before Veronica can even process the grief of losing her best friend, her father arrests a suspect – Lily's father Jake.

The arrest of the richest and most powerful man in town turns the community against Sheriff Mars. And when a drifter shows up and confesses to the murder, Keith is driven from office and publicly humiliated. Unable to deal with the stress, Veronica's mother starts drinking heavily and finally runs away from home. And Veronica is forced to choose between her rich friends and her father. She chooses Dad, and is immediately shunned by everyone she used to know.

Meanwhile, a new sheriff is sworn in, Jake Kane is released, and Veronica's father opens a small private detective agency to pay the bills. Veronica spends her free time helping Keith with his cases. But she refuses to back down in the face of her former friends' hostility, and even goes to one of their parties – where she is drugged and, while unconscious, raped.

Wow. That's a lot of great story material. Probably not enough for an entire season here, but it could get the average series through a half dozen episodes.

There was only one problem – all this great story material *happened before the pilot.*

That's right. When we first meet Veronica, it's been months since Keith lost his job and Veronica lost all her friends and Mom ran away. Even the rape is something of a distant memory.

So how does writer/creator Rob Thomas manage to convey this enormous amount of really crucial backstory? In classic detective novel fashion, through flashbacks narrated by world-weary private eye Veronica.

A classic technique – which in this case, I believe, really killed the show. Because everything that Veronica tells and shows us in flashback is much more interesting than anything that's going on in the forward action. Dad's got a case and it's got something to do with the Kane family, and maybe even with Veronica's mother. But as mildly intriguing as these hints may be, they can't begin to compare to the power of the scenes we never see of Veronica discovering her best friend murdered and everything that follows from there.

The effect is that even as we're watching the pilot – the very first episode of the series – it seems as if we've already missed all the good stuff, and we're seeing the brief "previously on *Veronica Mars*" that might run before the second-season premiere. There's a huge distancing effect that's almost impossible to bridge.

Please notice that I say *almost* impossible. There are people who loved and still love this show, many prominent critics among them. Although routinely reported as being on the bubble for cancellation, it did manage to last for three seasons. So some part of the audience was able to connect.

But what audience the show had seemed to be constant throughout its run – those who were devoted stuck with it; those who were indifferent to start with were never swayed to become regular viewers.

And I believe that one strong reason for that was the choice of storytelling structure. By setting so much of the show's story material in the past – and worse, by setting almost all of the really interesting stuff in the past – the creator robbed his own series of urgency, and in fact made what should have been wildly entertaining look like it was going to be hard work. If every new plot twist was going to require fifteen minutes of flashbacks to explain, was it really worth it to sit through another episode? Couldn't we just get the CliffsNotes instead?

(Now to be fair, asking a devoted audience to work to gain an deeper understanding of a show can be a powerful bonding tool between creator and viewer – just look at all the insane supplementary material they put out for *Lost*. But before you can capitalize on this kind of rabid fan devotion, you actually have to attract your initial audience. And you simply can't do that by saying "do a lot of hard work – it'll be worth it." You've got to make it worth it to them first.)

If the pilot of *Veronica Mars* had been structured differently, would the show have been a bigger success? Obviously there's no way to know that. Maybe the world wouldn't have been interested in a *film noir* detective series with a cute teenage blonde in the lead.

Am I saying you should avoid ambitious structural devices when you sit down to conceive your series? Absolutely not – it's the kind of thing that can set your script apart from a million other specs.

What I am saying is that if you do try playing with structure, if you experiment with alternate storytelling techniques, you need to have a really good reason for doing so, preferably one rooted in the franchise's essential conflicts. And you need to be aware of the effect your gimmicks can have on the overall emotional impact of your script.

The Pilot Story

You know your series. You've figured out your characters and how they're going to interact. You understand what your world is like and how your people will move around in it. You understand your conflicts and how they are going to power every story you tell.

Then there really is only one more question: What story should you tell?

Well, maybe there are really two more questions. Because before you can decide what story to tell, you need to choose which kind of story it's going to be.

In a pilot, you've got two ways to go – you can write a *premise pilot* or you can stick with a *regular episode*. Both have their advantages and disadvantages, and we'll discuss how to choose a way to go. But first, we should define our terms.

A *premise pilot* directly sets up the franchise by showing the series of events that puts the characters and conflicts in motion. A *regular episode* pilot is just what it sounds like – although it is the first written, its content is such that it could conceivably be aired at any point in the season.

Lost, obviously, is a premise pilot. It begins with the crash of that airliner on the island. Nothing that happens in the series could conceivably come before that episode. (Leaving out all that flashback material, obviously…) *Mad Men*'s pilot is a regular episode. It picks up with Don Draper in the middle of what will obviously be a typical kind of crisis for him – in this case, the need to come up with a new ad campaign for Lucky Strikes cigarettes now that Reader's Digest has declared tobacco to be a carcinogen.

For most of us as writers, there is a great temptation to go with a premise pilot. We are telling a story, and where better to start that than with the beginning?

Beyond that basic impulse is one simple fact: A premise pilot seems much, much easier than a regular episode.

Remember, what you're doing in the pilot is establishing the characters, situations and, most important, conflicts that are going to drive your next hundred stories. You've got to introduce all these elements to your audience and do it in a way that feels natural. That's easy if the characters are also being introduced to these elements at the same time.

Let's look at that *Lost* pilot again. One of the first episode's primary jobs is to tell the audience what the conflicts are and why they are this way. If we started *Lost* with a "regular episode," we'd meet the castaways already on the island and struggling to survive. We'd have to invent an episodic story that would give the characters a reason to demonstrate who they are. We'd have to explain how they got here, why they can't leave, and what they're hoping to do about it.

That takes a lot of skill. Because everyone on this island knows exactly why they're on the island and why they can't leave. They've all tried various ways to get off or to look for help. And because they've all been through this before, there's absolutely no reason why they would proceed to explain any of it to each other.

This is the hardest part of writing a "regular episode" pilot – because it really isn't a regular episode. It's the very first episode, and everything you can take for granted in later episodes needs to be explained here. But in real life – and in good drama – people don't go around explaining the everyday facts of their shared lives. You'll really never hear anyone say, "Bob, as you know I'm your brother" or "Remember when I first came to this precinct from that small town sheriff's office and you told me I'd never last five minutes here?"

That's the great appeal of the premise pilot. There's so little to explain. And in a show with a complex set-up, it's almost a requirement. If you're going to create a show about a regular family that gets turned into superheroes, you're going to want to show us how this happens. We need to see what caused this change in order to believe it. And we've got to see what the family was like before they were hit by lightning or doused in chemicals to understand how their lives have changed afterwards. In a show like *The Riches*, which depends on a complex series of events to set up its franchise, it's almost impossible to imagine how it could all be conveyed in exposition – especially since the only people who know the truth have no reason to explain it to each other and no one outside the family can know about it.

All of which seems to be a pretty convincing set of arguments for using the set-up of your franchise as the story for your pilot. And if setting up the conflicts in your franchise was the only purpose of the pilot episode, there would be no reason to do anything else.

But a pilot doesn't merely start the story of the series – the way the first episode of a mini-series would. It also sets the template for every episode that's going to follow. And this is where the premise story can get you into serious trouble. Because the conflicts that play out in setting up the franchise are not necessarily the same as those that will come into effect once everything has been put in motion. You can spend your entire pilot showing how a mild-mannered scientist is blasted by radiation and turns into an angry green monster and how that makes it impossible for him to keep his job and his home. And that may make for a compelling story on its own. But it doesn't tell the audience where the series is going in week two – or in week two hundred. There's no way of knowing that the scientist will go on the run, and every week he'll meet and help a new set of people, only to have to flee again once the monster inside him comes out.

This is why the premise pilot is so much harder than it initially seems – it's not only the premise of the story that has to be set up, but the franchise of the series. Which means that an effective premise pilot has to do two things at the same time: It's got to work as the first episode, starting the story, and it's got to succeed as a regular episode, giving a feel for what will be in every other hour.

To do that you've got to craft a pilot story that will allow you to set up the series' ongoing conflicts while still working the same way the next ones will. That's the approach my partner and I took with *Ella Clah*, for example. Every week Ella would be solving a murder that took her between the reservation and Albuquerque, so we gave her one in the pilot. The *story* of that script was about Ella being forced to deal with her family and culture, but the *plot* we used to drive that story was exactly the kind of crime she'd be solving every week. So that when you were done with the pilot you'd understand why you wanted – or didn't want – to come back the following week.

The one thing that is really crucial for your pilot story, whether premise or regular episode, is that it stay *simple*. A complicated story full of twists and turns is going to eat up pages – and you really need to devote as many of those pages as possible to establishing your characters and conflicts. If your pilot is some kind of mystery – and let's fact it, most shows are in one way or another, whether your protagonists are searching for a serial killer or the cause of a patient's illness or the truth in a case before the courts – this is not the time to uncover the centuries-old secrets of the Knights Templar and the Rosicrucians. (Unless, of course, your series is about uncovering centuries-old conspiracies…) You don't need thirty suspects and twists at the end of every scene, no matter how brilliant your plotting may be. Nobody is going to come back for week two of a series simply because they failed to guess the killer's identity. They're going to come back because they're fascinated by the characters and conflicts.

I can't think of any pilot that demonstrates this better than Stephen J. Cannell's script for *The Rockford Files*. Yes, it is nearly forty years old now, and if you watch the pilot you can see many ways in which it has become dated – the storytelling is slower than in any recent show, the wardrobe design is even more hideous than anything you can imagine, the long-lens car chases are as dull as action can ever be. But in terms of establishing a character and a franchise, this is still among the cleanest, sharpest pilots ever written.

(And the show continues to be held in high regard even among TV executives who otherwise can't imagine that the concept of television existed before they were born in 1997. When you pitch to a studio or network, you are often asked to compare your idea to an existing series – generally if you mention a show that ended before the turn of the millennium you have killed your chances. The only exceptions to that rule, the only genuinely old shows that would still receive an enthusiastic response as a model, were *The Rockford Files* and *Columbo*.)

The first thing you need to know about the *Rockford* pilot is that it is not a premise pilot. The second is that it easily could have been.

The latter might come as a surprise if you only have vague memories of watching the occasional episode in reruns when you were supposed to be doing your homework. Jim Rockford was a low-rent private eye who lived and worked out of a trailer by the beach in Malibu, right? What would you do in a premise pilot – show him buying the trailer? Shopping for ugly jackets?

Actually, *The Rockford Files* started out with a fairly elaborate premise. Several years back, Jim Rockford was arrested and wrongly convicted of armed robbery. He served five years in San Quentin, during which time his retired truck driver father never stopped fighting to prove his innocence. Finally he was successful, and Rockford was granted a full pardon by the governor. Now he's gone into business as a private eye, but because he wants to stay out of the way of the police, whom he still mistrusts – and, no doubt, for other, more personal reasons – he only takes cases that the cops have given up on.

If that description makes you think you've seen this concept somewhere else a little more recently, you have. In 2007, NBC premiered a series called *Life*, about a police detective who was framed for his friend's murder and sentenced to life in prison. In the pilot, the detective gets out of jail, wins a $50 million wrongful conviction lawsuit against the city of Los Angeles, and takes his old job back solving murders for the LAPD. During his years in prison, he's adopted a Zen philosophy that gives him a unique approach toward other people and to the cases he has to solve.

There are, of course, huge differences between the two series, and between the pilots. But one of the biggest is the amount of time *Life* spent delving into its own mythology. Detective Charlie Crews wasn't just framed – he was framed by a *conspiracy*. And he doesn't just solve the murders that come across his desk – he's trying to track down the identity of the mysterious cabal that framed him.

Of course, he *had* to do that. Because that was a major part of the pilot; the conspiracy was part of the show promised by the initial episode. But – at least in my opinion – it's also what kept the show from catching on. Crews was a great character, and when he was free to solve the crime of the week he was a blast to watch, as were his interactions with people who simply couldn't understand him. But when this show was commissioned, network television was in the grip of *Lost*-mania, and every series needed long, deep, intricate mysteries that would be resolved only after several seasons passed – if at all. As *Life*'s mythology grew ever more complicated, it became harder and harder for a casual viewer to get or stay involved. That meant that only the hardcore fans would watch and, as their number dwindled (as audiences inevitably do), there were no new viewers to replace them.

That was never going to be a problem with *The Rockford Files*. Cannell and co-creator Roy Huggins had no interest in using Jim Rockford's backstory for plot material. Its only purpose was to inform his character. It helps to explain why he is inevitably drawn to help the little guy up against much bigger forces, even when the bigger forces are able to pay better, and why he's such a soft touch for a sob story.

That's why there was no premise pilot for *The Rockford Files* – to start the first episode with Rockford's framing and forgiveness would be to make that mythology an essential part of the show. And that was never what the show was going to be about. In fact, after the first season you rarely heard about Rockford's time in prison, and very early on he stopped specializing in "closed" cases.

Which brings us back to the pilot that Cannell actually wrote. The one that's not a premise, but a "regular episode." And that is exactly what it is. If you were flipping channels and came across this, you could easily watch the whole thing and never realize it was the pilot. You might wonder why there seems to be a little more exposition about Rockford's past than usual – but just as easily you might not, because it is so skillfully woven into the fabric of the scenes.

What's impressive here, and what deserves to be studied as you are conceiving your own pilot story, is how well Cannell establishes every important aspect of the series as he joins it seemingly in progress. He's able to do this because he's crafted the story with exactly this in mind.

If you have 72 minutes to spare, it's worth pausing to watch this pilot right now. (It's available on DVD and, as of this writing, it is streamable from Netflix and who knows where else; it seems unlikely that it will become substantially less available over the next few years.) But if this is not convenient, let's take a moment to look at exactly what that pilot story is.

An old wino is strangled under Santa Monica pier. The police take a cursory glance at the case, but when they don't come across any leads they give up, tossing it into the closed file. Sarah Butler, the victim's daughter, can't stand the thought of her father's killer walking free, and when the cops refuse to help, she hires Rockford. The only lead she has seems insignificant at first – Sarah's loser brother has long wanted to go to medical school, but couldn't afford it. Now a wealthy widow who is a client of the pharmacy where he works has offered to pay his tuition – why? Rockford discovers that the widow, Mrs. Elias, became a multi-millionaire when her elderly groom dropped dead on their wedding night in Las Vegas. But there was no question that the death was anything but natural causes, and Rockford is ready to drop the case. Until Mrs. Elias's beefy friend Jerry Grimes starts following the detective and tries to assault him. Now Rockford knows that Mrs. Elias was mixed up in the murder – but there's absolutely no connection between any of the suspects and Sarah's father. What's going on?

That's it for the mystery. An old guy we care nothing about is killed in the teaser. We know who did it, even if our hero doesn't. (We see Jerry Grimes strangle the old man.) There's only one clue, and it leads directly to the people involved in the crime. There are no leads to follow, no shocking revelations, no second-act discovery of a cover-up that climbs all the way to the highest reaches of the police department. The only question the plot poses is just what the old wino has to do with what must have been a conspiracy to kill Mr. Elias years back and why he seemed to pose a threat to the murderers now.

I've written a lot of mystery stories in my career – hundreds, probably – and I have to say I've never attempted one that was so simple, so completely without twist or nuance or even suspects.

Maybe that's why Stephen J. Cannell became one of the most successful writer/producers in the history of television and I didn't. Because he understood that the story for the pilot of *The Rockford Files* had to be this simple. Because he understood what the show was really about – and it wasn't cool plot twists.

Instead of an elaborate crime story intended to dazzle the audience, Cannell crafted a deliberately simple mystery – albeit with a clever twist at the end – that he could use as a framework to hold together a series of scenes that were not really about the case, but were about Jim Rockford's life.

(A note: I keep giving Cannell full credit for the pilot, while the onscreen credit is split between Cannell for teleplay and "John Thomas James" – a pseudonym for co-creator Roy Huggins – for story. Huggins was one of the giants of dramatic television, and one of his biggest hits was the James Garner Western *Maverick*, which clearly provided the model for *Rockford*. Huggins was a major creative force in the early days of *The Rockford Files*, and I don't mean to diminish his contribution here; not knowing how the two writers actually divided the workload, I credit Cannell alone for the sake of simplicity.)

The genius of *The Rockford Files* was that the episodes were never really about the crime under investigation. Those plots were no more than an excuse to team Rockford up with a guest character who would annoy the hell out of him. And the pilot story was structured to function in exactly this way.

The primary dramatic thrust of the pilot story is not about Jim Rockford solving the murder. It's about Rockford refusing the case. He knows it's a loser, he doesn't believe there's anything to it, and he doesn't want to touch it. But Sarah Butler is insistent – he's her last chance, and she's not going to let him refuse.

So the first half of the pilot is one long back and forth between Rockford and Sarah. She comes to him for help; he tries to push her away by insisting on his rate (two hundred dollars a day plus expenses). She insists she's wealthy and writes him a check. He calls the bank and finds out she doesn't have the money to cover it. She offers to pay him in installments, he does the math for her, pointing out how long she'll be in debt.

These scenes must have felt particularly fresh when the show first aired, coming as it did in a TV schedule littered with private eyes who always did the right thing, constantly stood up for good, and never took a dime. But even now they crackle. The surface conflict as Sarah tries to find a way to get Rockford to help her is terrific on its own, but what really makes it work is the way it brings out the internal conflict in Jim Rockford that will drive the rest of the series – he's a smart, tough guy who knows too much to get dragged into the schemes of needy losers and wants to spend his life doing nothing but looking out for himself, but deep down he's got such a soft heart for these people that he can't stop himself from getting involved with them.

Even the scenes in which Rockford investigates the crime are much less about what he finds out than how he goes about the job. He puts on a pair of thick glasses and visits Mrs. Elias, pretending to be an admissions officer from the medical school where Sarah's brother has applied. He doesn't learn much; the scene's pleasure comes from his "disguise." (This, of course, was setting up a standard part of the franchise – Rockford would go "undercover" like this in many episodes.)

And when Rockford discovers that he's being followed, he hides out in burlesque house – who knew such things still existed in Los Angeles in the mid-'70s – goes into the bathroom, and waits for Jerry to come after him. But while he's waiting, he takes the soap dispenser off the wall and pours the liquid soap on the floor, so that when karate-instructor Jerry attempts a fancy flying kick, his feet go out from under him, he falls on his back, and Rockford is able to tie him up with his own belt after giving him a few quick kicks. "That's the trouble with you karate guys," Rockford says. "You always think the other guy is going to fight fair."

Jim Rockford is everything the TV private detective was supposed not to be – he was a coward who would back out of a fight every time he could, he was a cheat, he didn't care about "justice," and he was at constant war with himself over whether or not he should get involved in other people's problems. Most of all, he was a loser who knew he was never going to win.

And we know this all from the pilot. And we know it from the pilot because the pilot story allowed us to know it. We know it because the pilot story was structured to give us a series of scenes that would show it. If the story had been designed differently – if scene after scene had followed the unraveling of an intricate crime plot, if two acts had been devoted to seeing Rockford being put behind bars and then being pardoned, if the structure had existed with any other purpose than to allow scenes that would examine Rockford's character – we might never have seen *The Rockford Files*.

Because it doesn't matter how brilliant your series concept is, it doesn't matter how stark your conflicts or how original your characters. If your pilot story isn't designed and built to show them off, no one will ever know.

The Fun

The pilot for *Glee*, the biggest dramatic hit on any network in years, starts with a gymnastic, balletic workout by the high school cheer squad set to a bouncing hip-hop song. It's bright, loud, colorful, funny, exciting. And what does it have to do with the story that takes up the rest of the hour?

Nothing.

The show is about the members of the glee club and the teacher who leads them. It's not about cheerleaders. So why is this here? This is the opening scene of the very first episode of the series – shouldn't it actually have something to do with what the show is going to about?

Well, yes.

And no.

Because creator Ryan Murphy isn't selling the story here, or the characters or the conflicts. He's not even telling us anything about the concept.

What he's doing us is selling us *the fun*.

Despite my clever use of italics, *the fun* is not actually an official TV business term. But it should be. When I talk about *the fun* of a pilot, what I mean is that one element that's going to set your project apart from every other script. It's the hook that's going to keep audiences coming back week after week. It's the special thing that you're going to offer that no one else can.

And it's essential that it be all over your pilot.

What's the *fun* of *Glee*? It's those bright, loud, colorful, funny, exciting, moving musical numbers. They set it apart from every other show that's on the air. And you can bet that the pilot is going to be filled with them.

But there's a problem at the beginning of the show. Until about halfway through the pilot script, the glee club is in terrible shape. That's basically the point of the entire pilot story. So you can't have a brilliant musical number at the beginning of the hour and then try to explain why the glee club is in such dire straits. Thus the cheerleading session, which announces in the very first seconds exactly why you should stick around and watch for the next hour. If you like this, you're going to love what comes next.

You don't need to start your pilot off with a hard-sell moment like this. You don't necessarily have to grab your readers by the lapel in the first line and hold on for dear life. Some scripts are actually better served by a slower opening.

But as you are structuring your story, as you're writing your script, you do need to keep in mind at all times that you've got to put the *fun* in – whatever that is for your particular pilot.

That *fun* is going to define your series to most of the people who watch it. You need them to fall in love with your characters, true, but without that hook, that little something that is unique to your show, they're never going to stick around long enough to get interested in the people.

If you are writing a pilot about a bunch of scientists who accidentally open up a rip in the time space continuum and let dinosaurs into 21st-century America, you may have all kinds of lofty themes in mind about scientific progress or personal responsibility or the nature of civilization. And ideally your audience will see past the surface excitement and join your debate.

But first, they want to see the dinosaurs in Manhattan. They want to see the pterodactyl nesting in the Chrysler Building, the Tyrranosaurus Rex stomping through Grand Central Station, the raptors chasing investment bankers through the corridors of Goldman Sachs. (Although in that case I'd bet on the bankers to win...)

And they don't want to wait until act four to see it.

Your audience has been sold a series about dinosaurs in America, and that's what you need to give them. If you hold off on the rip in the space-time continuum and don't let the first monster through until the end of act three, your audience will be long gone. Because what they'll be seeing is not a show about dinosaurs in the modern world; it's a show about a bunch of scientists blathering about the danger and excitement of scientific experimentation – or whatever it is you're using to fill those pages until your story actually kicks in. And they're going to assume that this is what the show is going to be like every week – *because that's what a pilot is.*

(This, by the way, is one more reason to be wary of the premise pilot. Since your *fun* is going to be inextricably linked to your premise, you can't really get it going until that premise has kicked in.)

This is not just the case with high-concept pilots. If your series is about a brilliant private detective who happens to suffer from obsessive-compulsive disorder, we want to see both sides of this right up top – we want to see him suffering from OCD and we want to see how this helps or hinders his detective skills. If you're doing something like *CSI*, in which technicians are able to make astonishing judgments by looking at bits of forensic evidence, you've got to show us something of this right away. If you've got a cop from Alabama who's a fish out of water because he's just transferred to Chicago, we need to get him to the Windy City no later than the end of act one.

Now you may be thinking that this point is so obvious that you should be insulted I think I need to bring it up. Of course you're going to remember to put in your pilot the one thing that excited you about the project in the first place.

But it's very easy to say that when your concept is just a concept. Once you get into the actual business of plotting your pilot story, you often start to forget little things like, say, the point.

That's because crafting any story is hard, and crafting a pilot story is much, much harder. You will find yourself struggling just to come up with a set of twenty-four beats over four or five or six acts that begin to accomplish even half of what you need to get done in this script. You'll get to that all-important mid-point break thinking that you've got it all put together, and then realize that you haven't found a way to introduce one of your most important conflicts, or that while your story may be moving, your protagonist has not actually done anything in those first acts. And you're going to have to rip it apart and start all over again.

When you do finally get a story that works, when all your beats mesh together and the conflicts are all making sense and your plot is satisfyingly unpredictable, you will be faced with an almost irresistible temptation to hold on to this version and start writing the script. And when you realize that in making the story work you've put off getting to the *fun* for thirty pages, you decide it's really better that way. It's like a monster movie – you never want to show the creature the first couple of times it attacks. Or you'll find some other way to justify the decision… because the story was so hard to get done you can't bear the idea of starting over again.

But you need to. We live in a cluttered world right now. We've got a million distractions pulling us in every direction. If you want the reader's attention – or, later, the viewer's – you've got to demand it. And you've got to give us something that's going to keep us there until you're ready to let us go. Don't promise us that things will get exciting by the end; make it exciting *now*.

In other words, bring on the *fun*.

Why This Show Why Now?

Many years ago, the head of CBS went to Stan Lee, the legendary founder of Marvel Comics and co-creator of *Spiderman, The Fantastic Four, The Hulk, Iron Man* and a zillion other comic book characters, and asked him for a pilot about a female super-hero. Stan was partnered on the project with a team of producers my partner and I had worked with before, and they came to us to create the character and work up a pitch.

(Actually, the pilot we were originally asked to develop was based on the Marvel Comics character The Black Widow. But this was a time when Stan was on the outs with Marvel management, and no one could figure out exactly who controlled which rights. So we created our own character, Silhouette, who was something of a cross between the Black Widow and Richard Sapir and Warren Murphy's Remo Williams.)

We pitched our concept to the head of the network, and he liked it a lot, sending us off to come up with the pilot story. We pitched that to him, and he approved us to go to script. We wrote the draft and turned it in and waited for word. But we were feeling pretty good about the project, because this was something the network had specifically asked for, and we were pretty sure we'd delivered what they were looking for.

And then we got the call from the network. They only had one question:

Why this show, and why now?

In other words, you tell us why we should make a show about a female superhero and put it on our network this season.

I was astonished. More than that, I was angry. Because there was only one answer to that question that made any sense to me: Why this show? *Because you asked for it!* Why now? *Because you just asked for it!* So why are you now demanding that we justify the thing that you called us up to do for you?

That wasn't exactly the answer we gave, but it was probably pretty close. And *Silhouette* went away.

I wasn't able to give the right answer because I didn't understand what the question meant. I was too wrapped up in the script itself, in the characters and conflicts, to look at the bigger picture.

But it's been a lot of years since then, and I've watched a lot of TV seasons come and go, seen some excellent shows struggle through a season or two while others – some just as good, some much worse – become the kinds of hits that dominate all of pop culture. And what I've observed is that it's not enough that a show be good for it to become a huge hit, it's got to be *necessary*.

What I mean by that is that a series has to speak to its time. It's got to have something to say about some aspect of the world, it's got to resonate with the issues that people are obsessing over.

Don't get me wrong – I'm not talking about doing an "issue" show like a *Lou Grant* or *I'll Fly Away*. (In fact, as evidence you shouldn't be doing an issue show is the fact that I had to reach back decades just to find a couple of fairly identifiable examples...) You don't need to be lecturing about the Big Problems That Confront Our Society Today.

But you do need to be connecting with them. This really hit home for me when I was watching the pilot for J. J. Abrams' science fiction show *Fringe*. A taut, weird thriller, the show follows the adventures of a super-secret, super-special FBI strike force as they investigate crimes involving "fringe science." What was clear in that pilot was that most of these crimes were going to involve a massive global conspiracy called "the Pattern." (Actually, it turned out to be even bigger than global, as it was established in later seasons that the cabal emanated from a parallel Earth...)

To put it in TV-pitch shorthand, it was *The X-Files*, but with extreme science instead of extraterrestrials as the focus of the stories.

The pilot was well-written, well-directed, cast and acted. It gained a devoted, if smallish, following and has stayed on the air for several years. In other words, it's done pretty much what the major networks have come to expect from a well-executed genre show.

That wasn't the case with *The X-Files*. After a first year in which it struggled, the series began to catch on in its sophomore season and quickly rose to be one of the biggest hits on any network. More than that, though, it became one of the signature shows of its time, its catchphrases repeated in everyday conversations, its ideas embraced, imitated, and parodied on every level of the popular culture.

That's not going to happen with *Fringe*, no matter how long it stays on the air. It will entertain its audience, one assumes it will make money for everyone involved, it will no doubt serve as a launch pad for a bunch of careers, but it will never *matter* in the way *The X-Files* did.

This is not a reflection on the quality of either show, just on what they have to say about the times in which they aired. *The X-Files* premiered in 1993 and saw its ratings climb as the decade went on, its themes – boldly stated in its opening credits – of "the truth is out there" and "trust no one" becoming popular catchphrases all through the '90s.

Why did those paranoid ideas seem so compelling at the time? I have a theory. The '90s were a time of great prosperity and excitement – the stock market was exploding, the tech industry was churning out new miracles every day, there seemed to be high-paying jobs for everyone who wanted one, and for those who aimed a little higher, it was possible to create a business on Monday, land millions in venture capital on Tuesday, go public on Wednesday and retire a billionaire by the weekend. The world was at peace – if you ignored little corners of Eastern Europe – America's greatest enemy had disappeared off the face of the Earth, and the future seemed to have no limits.

So not exactly the dark and frightened times you'd expect to generate dark conspiracy theories, right? Except that while everything seemed to be going so well, no one really knew why. Tech businesses were booming, but you couldn't tell what they did or why they were successful. Silicon Valley was exploding, but for most of the country computers were still mysterious devices whose use they were still trying to figure out. Even the fall of the Soviet Union seemed to have happened with no real explanation – one minute Ronald Reagan was saying "tear down this wall," the next David Hasselhoff was singing on the rubble.

After all those years of trouble and strife, it couldn't be that easy, could it? There had to be a *reason* why everything was booming. And while some might have counseled that it would be better just accept the good times without question, even those who tried to accept the advice couldn't help feeling that if they didn't understand why things were going so well, they'd never be able to tell when they were about to turn bad again.

And so, people were searching for explanations. There had to be a reason why everything was going so well. There had to be a plan. But if there was, it was a plan that was being kept hidden from them.

A *conspiracy*.

What *The X-Files* offered when it aired was an explanation. Its message was that even if things seemed random and inexplicable, there actually was someone out there controlling everything. And it was just as dark and scary and evil as you feared in your wildest speculations. The show tapped into a zeitgeist that was so deep that most of the people who felt it weren't even aware they did – but they fell in love with the show that spelled it out for them.

By the time *Fringe* appeared in 2008, the country was in a very different state. The economy had gone to hell, the housing bubble burst. People had lost their life's savings and were at risk of losing their homes. America was fighting two wars, and most people had no real idea why. We'd been attacked by terrorists for reasons we didn't understand, and we had no idea if or when they

– or someone else we didn't see coming – would strike again. And the rest of the world was no better off. Other countries seemed to be slipping into bankruptcy, and then anarchy. It was so insane that supertankers were being hijacked by pirates off the coast of Africa. Pirates – in the 21st century.

If there once had been a great fear that things were too good and there was no reason for it, that was long gone. The fear now was a lot simpler – chaos. The country and the world were falling apart, and no one seemed to have the slightest idea what to do about it.

And then came *Fringe*, which posited an international cabal of villains who were secretly manipulating the world and actually responsible for terrible things happening across the face of the planet.

But a funny thing had happened over the years. The idea of a global conspiracy wasn't scary anymore. In fact, it was comforting. *Thank God, at least someone knows what the hell is going on out there!*

Now I'm not saying that the viewers who watched the *Fringe* pilot and never bothered to check in with subsequent episodes, or who drifted away after the first couple of weeks, had a conscious thought that they no longer suspected there was some kind of sinister conspiracy running the world and therefore they weren't going to bother with this series. Audience response rarely works that way.

But I know that when I watched the pilot, I was left with the sense that the series, no matter how smart or well done, just didn't have anything to say to me. From the very first mention of "the Pattern," the entire conspiracy angle seemed dated and unimportant. And even though I'd enjoyed some of Abrams' shows in the past while being constantly aware of their flaws – I sat through five years of *Alias* and *that's* what the freaking Rambaldi device was all about? – I just couldn't see investing any more time or effort in this one. It was not the right show for the right time.

Which brings me back to poor *Silhouette* and the question that ended her life before it began: Why this show why now?

And in a way, I have to say that my answer wasn't too far off the mark – "You ordered the damn thing – you tell me." Because even if the heads of the network couldn't explicitly articulate why they thought it was the right time to try a female superhero, something had led them to the belief. They did know, but they needed me to tell them.

What I should have told them, what I should have been able to articulate, was that this was exactly the right time for a female superhero. It was the mid-'90s, when third-wave feminism had leapt from academia to gender politics and finally into pop culture. This movement, like the earlier iterations, was about female empowerment – but it was different, too. Because this wasn't about being "just as good as men" or "just like men." Earlier waves of feminism had demanded that women stop being patronized, stop being treated like little girls and be allowed to become fully functioning members of society.

Third-wave was all about the girl. It was a movement that said "we don't have to stop being girls to be as good as you – or better." It was the time of Riot Grrrls and Bitch Magazine and sex-positive feminism. Courtney Love and kinderwhore fashion and Bikini Kill.

The young, tough girl who took the iconography of belittlement – baby doll dresses, patent leather shoes – and turned it into armor, who controlled her own sexuality and her own destiny and didn't care what anyone said about it – she was all over pop music, all over the fashion world, and one way or another she was going to break through into television.

There was an audience ready for a kick-ass female hero, and they were ready right then.

That's what I should have said.

But I didn't understand the question, and I didn't think through the answer, and because of that *Silhouette* went away.

But that tough girl superhero? The world *was* ready for her. And it wasn't long before *Xena, Warrior Princess* premiered and almost instantly eclipsed *Hercules*, the show it had been spun off from. And not much longer until *Buffy, The Vampire Slayer* and *Alias*.

Because they were the right shows at the right time.

Your Pilot, The Business And The Future

As I start on this final chapter this morning, word comes that another network has purchased another spec pilot. That's at least half a dozen for this development season, more than any year previous. Next January the tally will probably be even higher. After that, anything could happen – the networks could reimpose control, refusing to buy anything they hadn't developed in house. Or the entire development system could collapse. Networks might simply stop commissioning the bulk of their scripts, instead sending out vague feelers to the big agencies about the kinds of shows they're hoping to see, and waiting for the wave of specs to flow in.

That last option might sound improbable, as multinational companies don't generally like to outsource their product development process. But there's going to be an economic imperative – commissioning a hundred pilot scripts costs the networks millions of dollars; hiring a couple of readers to plow through thousands of specs will cost thousands. Maybe hundreds, if they get really cheap.

There's one thing you need to understand about your own pilot script:

It's not going to be one of them.

I don't mean to be negative here, and this is certainly not meant as any kind of criticism of your talent, which I sincerely hope is huge and shining.

But as the market for spec pilots expands, the pool of people writing them is going to grow even faster. Most of the specs sold this year have been written by lower-level producers on current shows.

They're going to be joined by every working writer in the business once networks stop buying pitches and start with the scripts. You're going to be competing with hundreds of experienced pros who have an inside track on what the buyers want, and who have a track record of being able to deliver what they promise.

So where does that leave you? Back on the outside, trying desperately to get someone to read your script?

For the moment, yes. And as I'm sure you already know, this is not a place you want to be. As long as you're standing on the wrong side of the door, holding out your script and politely asking to be admitted, they are never going to open it for you.

You need them to invite you in. You need to make them *want* to invite you in.

And while I wish this wasn't the case, your script, no matter how brilliant, isn't going to do that. *They don't want to read another script.*

So what do you do? The first thing is to come up with a reason why they'll want to meet with you.

Diablo Cody, screenwriter of *Juno* and creator of Showtime's *United States of Tara*, did this better than anyone. How did she do it? First, she went "undercover" as a stripper. Then she wrote about it, first on a blog, then in a book. And then she went out with her scripts. And I am sure there wasn't an executive in town who wouldn't meet with her. All the men wanted to imagine what she looked like naked; all the women wanted to see if she would look better naked than them.

Now it's important to say that this only got her through the door. The vast successes she's accrued since then wouldn't have happened if she didn't have the talent to show once she was in.

But you've got that talent, right? So how can you get them to open that door so you can prove it?

Sorry to say, I think taking off your clothes for money is off the table. These things tend to work only once.

But if your day job is putting out oil well fires, I'm pretty sure there isn't an exec who won't take the meeting. Or if you're an astronaut. If you wrestle crocodiles or work the line for Eric Ripert or masterminded an art heist from a major museum. If, in other words, you live a life that 20- and 30-something TV executives like to fantasize about. They'll meet with you because they want to hear your story – and then you'll have the chance to tell them your *story*.

But what if you don't lead an exciting life? What if the most exhilarating thing you ever do is the one thing you want to do – write? The last person any development executive wants to meet is another writer.

Then you've got to give them a reason to want your project. Not in the "when they read this, they'll all be bidding on it" kind of reason. I mean the "I don't know what the hell this is but if I don't grab it before that other guy I'll lose my job" kind.

And there's only one thing that's going to give them that reason. An audience.

It doesn't have to be a huge following. Tens, maybe hundreds of thousands of people on the internet – that's not all that hard to do. And it will tell development executives that you are bringing them a proven property.

But here's the catch:

You're not going to get this following with a script. It's just not going to happen.

This is something that's easier for aspiring comedy writers – look at *Shit My Dad Says*, a CBS sitcom based on a series of funny tweets. Because you can be funny in 140 characters – it's a lot harder to convey a drama that way.

No, to get attention for your spec pilot online, I'm afraid there's only one option. You're going to have to make it.

I know a lot of you will reject this thought right away. You're writers, not filmmakers.

But what do you think a showrunner is? If you ever get a series up and running and you are lucky enough to be running it, you will be responsible for all aspects of the production, financial and creative. So why not prove you can do it now?

Because you can. The technology is there. Professional quality camera and editing equipment are available as low-cost consumer goods. Odds are you already have them. Amateurs can create high-end special effects on their laptops. And once you're done, you can distribute it essentially for free on the Web.

I'm not going to lie to you – even though it's financially viable, it's going to be hard. You're going to have to find actors, crew members, composers. You're going to have to shepherd this whole project through, or find someone you can trust who will do it with you.

But this country is full of talented people who are desperate for a chance to show what they can do. Desperate for a chance just to work in the field they love, even if you can't afford to pay. As Roger Corman once said to me while I was working on a project for him, "I keep worrying that I'll run out of film students to exploit, but there seems to be a never-ending supply."

Of course there's no guarantee that even if you manage to produce your pilot, anyone will want to see it. People may hate it or, worse, be completely indifferent. And without some kind of following, it just becomes a spec DVD you're trying to get people to watch.

But once you've gone down this path, you're living in a world without gatekeepers. If you believe strongly enough in your project, you can keep it going. You can make a second episode. You can make a season. And if it's any good, it will gain an audience. And it will get you through the door.

And even if it doesn't – you've made a TV series.

And wasn't that the idea all along?

Acknowledgments

This book is a product of my quarter century in the TV business, and there's no way I can begin to thank all the writers, producers and executives who taught me the lessons I've tried to pass along here.

It was Tod Goldberg who convinced me to write this book, even if he has no memory of the conversation. Joshua Malkin and Anna Weinstein gave me brilliant ideas after volunteering for the miserable job of reading a first draft. Jann Nyffeler saved me from embarrassing myself on more than a couple of occasions.

And without Lee Goldberg this book simply could not exist. He was my partner in every one of the pilots I wrote for the networks, and for the three hundred hours of television we wrote and produced. Anything good in here is probably as much his as mine. I just got around to writing it down first.

Made in the USA
San Bernardino, CA
10 August 2017